THE CRUISING MATE'S HANDBOOK

THE CRUISING MATE'S HANDBOOK

A Guide to Good Crewing

Joyce Sleightholme

ADLARD COLES NAUTICAL

Adlard Coles *Nautical*
An imprint of A & C Black (Publishers) Ltd
35 Bedford Row, London WC1R 4JH

Previously published as *The Sea Wife's Handbook* by
Angus & Robertson 1970
Second edition 1976
This edition published by
Adlard Coles 1991

British Library Cataloguing in Publication Data

Sleightholme, Joyce
    The Cruising mate's handbook.
    1. Yachting
    I. Title
797.1246

ISBN 0-229-11868-2

Phototypeset by Computape (Pickering) Ltd, North Yorkshire
Printed and bound in Great Britain by
Hartnolls Ltd, Bodmin, Cornwall

CONTENTS

FOREWORD

Ideally, when two people make up the permanent crew of a cruising yacht, each should be as competent as the other. Joyce Sleightholme encourages this attainment with easily understandable advice and examples; she has a wealth of knowledge and beside her, a skilled skipper.

Until the cruising mate can achieve equal status with the skipper she/he is going to miss many of the rewards of sailing. At first there may be apprehension; then after the manoeuvre, passage or landfall has been successfully accomplished, there will be a glow of satisfaction that, whatever the anxieties or privations entailed, it will have been worth it. Reviewing a passage after arrival in a fresh anchorage can sometimes be the best part of it, but each new experience brings knowledge and confidence. Happy hours of planning the next cruise during the winter months require an appreciation of the sea-going hurdles involved and a knowledge of the capabilities of the yacht and her crew.

Sailing and cruising bring one solitude with the elements, freedom from the crowds and give freedom to make one's own decisions. To be on watch during the dark hours aboard a small vessel forging along with a fair wind, the masthead swinging through the stars, the landfall still beyond the horizon ahead, and one's mate asleep below can bring joyous elation to the watch keeper. Go on, help yourself.

Susan Hiscock
Yarmouth, Isle of Wight

PREFACE

While this book is dedicated to those sailing women who find themselves – by accident or design – tackling the job of cruising mate to their skipper husband or partner, the subject matter applies equally to any novice irrespective of age or sex who goes to sea in that capacity. The demands of a sailing cruiser at sea make no concessions; the job is the same.

The authoress at the helm of her Rival 32.

1 WOMEN AND CRUISING

Just a few generations ago cruising was very much a man's domain not only because it was considered 'unsuitable' for women but because boats and rigging were heavier and out of a woman's sphere physically. Today's cruising yachts are lighter, more sophisticated and need far less in the way of weight and muscle to sail them. Despite this the vast majority of women are apparently introduced to offshore sailing by boyfriends or husbands. This is changing, of course, as more and more women discover it for themselves, proving once and for all that sailing is for everyone.

In the world of cruising under sail, however, sailing wives remain the female majority, but just how deeply involved in the sailing they become is another matter. Some stay on the fringes seeing only the discomforts and none of the rewards. Some remain fair weather sailors who quite enjoy the nice bits. Others regard the cruiser as a type of holiday home and voluntarily leave the sailing to the men. Many more women, while concentrating on the domestic role, become deckhands whenever necessary, learning only as much as may be needed, not wishing to progress any further; a kind of dual-role crew in fact.

It is to take sailing wives and crews beyond that stage that this book is written. The progress from crew to mate in a family sailing cruiser is a short step, but one which offers huge rewards in terms of both pleasure and safety – because the typical situation in which a husband/skipper is the sole repository of skill and knowledge aboard a boat is a potential risk. He has only to fall and break a wrist, get a touch of food poisoning or become disabled in some way, and the whole crew is threatened.

Best of all, though, is the co-skipper relationship. More and more nowadays couples are starting together from scratch, enrolling in the same courses of instruction, choosing a boat together in joint ownership and thereafter sharing their mistakes and successes. Usually, and with the woman's consent, it seems to be the man who acts as nominal skipper since no boat can have two at once, but the end result is one of harmony and efficiency.

A boat can be jointly owned by two or more men, two or more women;

whatever the arrangement it is the duties of the mate that we are concerned with. The sea makes the same demands upon all small ships no matter what the sex or the competence of the crew may be. A safe boat is a well-crewed boat and a competent mate is the heart of a good crew.

The appeal of sailing

If you are a beginner, sailing can be either a revelation and make you eager to know more about it, or it can make you very reluctant to go again. A sparkling sail on a warm day is one thing, a grim slog on a chilly day under lowering skies is another; but if you decide to persevere then both become part of the same thing. It is the constant change, the alternation between ever-changing facets, fair winds and foul, fair tide and contrary, sunshine and greyness, night and day, that contribute to the great fascination of cruising. As a mode of transport a small sailing vessel has little to commend it; as an antidote to the stresses and cares of the daily grind it has everything.

Unless you are willing to take an active part in handling the boat, which for a woman means looking beyond the domestic element, sailing on passage can become very boring, with long hours just sitting and watching the waves go by. Once you involve yourself a little more deeply though, a simple passage of even a few hours becomes fascinating. Your departure may be dictated by the height of the tide or the direction of the currents; your course may be shaped to make best use of the wind direction; progress is recorded on the chart to avoid rocks and shoals; the distant blue shape of the land is searched for recognizable features which are then the focal points for compass bearings; and ongoing throughout there is the constant adjusting and trimming of sails as speed rises and falls. An arrival, even after a simple passage, always seems like a triumph; a satisfaction shared by everyone who has had a hand in it.

The mate's place

In a large yacht with numerous crew the mate is the second-in-command. The captain decides, the mate executes, organizing the crew and attending to detail. The mate is, in effect, the deputy skipper who is well qualified to do the skipper's job. In family cruisers with a crew consisting of parents and children the skipper, invariably the husband, not only has to decide how best to navigate the boat to the next port of call, and know when to stay in shelter and when to go, but needs also to attend to the myriad tasks of maintaining the rigging and machinery. The skipper should have enough experience to run the boat safely and efficiently for the good of all.

The mate may be a sailing friend of equal experience in which case no more need be said. Or the mate may be a very keen teenager who, though lacking experience, is always willing to tackle any job that comes along. More usually, though, the mate is the female partner. She provisions the ship and cooks the meals, keeps some sort of order below decks and shares the decisions. Knowing her skipper and his ability as a yachtsman she may also temper his wilder enthusiasms and question the wisdom of choosing this destination in favour of that. She shares the watchkeeping when on a passage between ports, thus allowing the skipper to get proper rest. She is a competent helmswoman and well able to keep the boat on a steady course whatever the conditions while he is busy with a vital bit of navigation. When entering a harbour she does not need

Light air sailing. The helmswoman is sitting on the lee side so that she can watch the trim of the headsail and get the best performance from the boat.

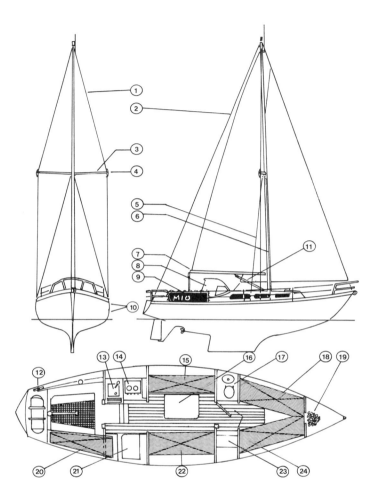

Fig 1a Parts of a yacht.

 1. Cap shroud
 2. Backstay
 3. Crosstree or spreader
 4. Sail-saver
 5. Starboard aft lower shroud
 6. Starboard fore lower shroud
 7. Boom
 8. Pram hood
 9. Spray dodger
10. Topsides
11. Boom kicking strop
12. Quarter cleat

13. Sink and draining board
14. Cooker
15. Port saloon berth
16. Saloon table
17. Toilet and washbasin/shower
18. Port forward berth
19. Anchor chain locker
20. Quarter berth
21. Chart table
22. Starboard saloon berth
23. Oilskin hanging locker
24. Starboard forward berth

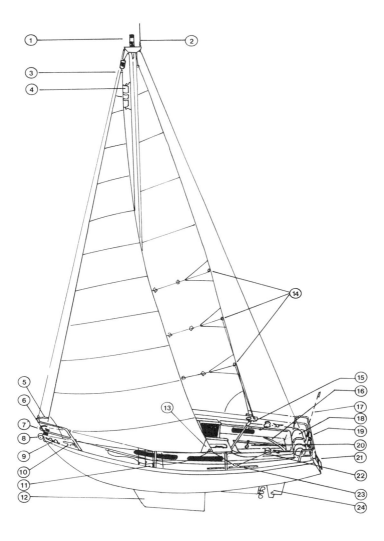

Fig 1b

1. Tricolour navigation light
2. VHF aerial
3. Head of sail
4. Radar reflector
5. Bow pulpit
6. Tack of sail
7. Roller jib drum
8. Anchor/mooring fairlead
9. Port/starboard rope fairleads
10. Mooring cleat
11. Lower and cap shrouds
12. Ballast keel
13. Clew of sail
14. Reefing pennants
15. Mainsheet
16. Tiller
17. Dan-buoy staff
18. Liferaft
19. Lifebuoy and stern pulpit
20. Engine gear control
21. Stern ladder
22. Sheet winch
23. Jib sheet fairlead
24. Rudder and skeg

to be told where to hang out the fenders, where to rig lines ready for use or, having nipped ashore, how to make them fast. She may have no desire to take over as skipper, but in the event of his injury or illness she could do just that.

All of this is fine provided you have the experience behind you. Unfortunately the husband–wife teacher–pupil arrangement is not always the best. The learning-to-drive syndrome is well known. In such a case it is far better for the would-be mate to learn the rudiments of offshore crewing by spending a week at a good sailing school. Most men, though a little jealous of their nautical standing, are often all too appreciative of skilled assistance in a tight spot. What everyone should remember in the case of small boats and small crews is that it is positively unsafe for all the essential skills to be invested in only one person on board.

We cannot all start out as full blown mates, but even for a total beginner there should be goals to achieve. A surprising amount can be absorbed merely by being aboard a boat, moving around, knowing where things are kept and routine procedures for getting under way – such as taking off the sail cover, putting winch handles in their stowage pockets, perhaps stowing fenders and hoisting flags and burgees. This routine soon becomes familiar. Arrival procedures, inflating and launching the dinghy, remembering to switch on the radio for weather forecasts, stowing gear below so that it stays put at sea and locking up before leaving the boat, all are essential, simple common sense jobs which anyone can master.

This is basic crewing; next come the basic skill jobs such as coiling ropes properly, tying simple knots to secure the dinghy, hanging out fenders and so on. By this stage the mysteries of how a boat sails must be tackled. You soon become competent to adjust the trim of the sails, anticipate the effect of course alterations or changes in the wind direction. You will have learned how to use the sheet winches and know the difference between tacking and gybing, running before the wind and beating against it.

Much depends upon how keen you are to learn and how ready others are to instruct you; unless you show some interest nobody is going to bother. Quite early on you must learn how to steer by the compass so that you can hold the boat steady on course while the skipper is navigating, hoisting sails or doing one of a dozen other things.

If you have already learned how to sail a dinghy it will be a great asset, but it is not essential. You can learn just as well in your cruiser – perhaps more easily since you will have no fear of capsizing! Learn you must though, because there is not always time for a compass course to be set, and a good mate should be able to grab the helm and sail the boat at a moment's notice.

Having reached this stage many wife-mates are content. What with their galley role and perhaps small children to keep an eye on they have plenty to keep them occupied. Their contribution on deck is a valuable one so why involve themselves any deeper? But they can contribute even more by *having the ability* to do more even if they do not often use their extra skills. For instance, knowing how to cope with the engine, how to use the VHF radio, how to read a chart and plot a safe course, anchor the yacht, take compass and radio bearings, interpret weather forecasts; all usually fall within the skipper's lot, but if a mate also shares them, his or her understanding of the whole art of sailing is greatly enhanced.

Women make excellent navigators because their minds are usually more precise and better at combining a variety of small factors to arrive at a conclusion – which is what good housekeeping is all about. In terms of brute strength, there is little aboard a modern cruising yacht which is beyond the average woman's strength. Raising the anchor perhaps, lugging the deflated dinghy up on deck, getting the last pound of sheet load in on a winch – but even such jobs as these can tax a man's strength. I have refrained from quoting such names as Clare Francis, Dame Naomi James and other famous singlehanded women sailors because they are motivated differently, although they have proved beyond doubt that sailing is for everyone. The only sexist feature of sailing is that boats are referred to as 'she's'!

Panics and alarms

Despite newspaper accounts of yachting tragedies and the fact that in Britain the Royal National Lifeboat Institution devotes a large percentage of time to rescuing yachtsmen, the dangers of cruising are surprisingly slight – far less than those of motoring. In ninety per cent of all mishaps the trouble is caused by over-cockiness, unsuitable boats, lack of knowledge, or seasickness. A small cruiser – even if her crew are beginners – need not get into serious trouble so long as they do not try to bite off more than they can chew and learn all they can, all the time.

A typical gentle cruise at sea in a small family yacht is not too ambitious at first – or should not be. With a fortnight's holiday ahead a yacht might spend perhaps five or six days at sea and possibly make one night passage. The rest of the time will be spent pottering about, or ashore sightseeing, or swimming from some sandy beach. Of the total time there will probably be one or two days when the going is hard, wet and tough; but providing the crew have not set themselves an impossible itinerary and there is no need for a back-at-all-costs return passage, there is no reason why the yacht should ever be at sea in bad weather. She can day-hop from port to port or maybe make the odd day-night-day passage if the weather is very settled. If bad weather threatens she holes up somewhere if it is possible to do so safely, her crew knowing full well that she need not be driven to sea due to shortage of time. At all costs it is the safety of the ship and crew that matter most, not how far she can go in the time or how brilliant the skipper may prove himself to be in a gale. Hard weather experience should come by degrees.

This type of sailing is for pleasure and that means the pleasure of all on board, children included. Of course there will be the unpleasant periods, but the thing to remember is that every small boat crew has a stamina limit. No matter how much the boat can take it is the crew that sets the pace, and once a crew begins pushing beyond its limits it is taking unnecessary risks. A sensible mate can do a great deal to regulate the pace. Skippers often feel the compulsion to press on, to keep to a planned holiday schedule as if the rest of the crew expect it and will be disappointed with less, with fewer places visited in the time available. These same skippers may be secretly relieved to know that others aboard would far rather spend another day in a nice place. Boats that are sailed within the limits of crew competence and stamina rarely get into trouble.

Entering a new harbour is always exciting, often a little tense, and the mate must think ahead of the jobs which may need doing and which a preoccupied skipper may forget.

Seasickness – the Achilles heel

Seasickness is the Achilles heel of sailing and the more one anticipates it the more prone one is likely to become. Some people are affected more than others, but it is a fact that those who have nothing to keep them occupied are harder hit than those who are absorbed in the running of the boat. Briefly, motion sickness is caused by disturbance in the balancing system of the inner ear, which is why the effects occur more rapidly when you are down below and subjected to boat motion than when you are aware of the horizon, clouds, distant land and so on, which act as steady reference points for the brain.

Anyone who is prone to seasickness should take their tablets (see later) a couple of hours before sailing, stay on deck until it is time to turn in for the watch below, and lie down immediately. Provided you do not try to cook a meal in the early stages of the sea passage the odds are that you will get your sea-legs, or sea tummy at any rate, after a few hours and thereafter be unaffected.

Seasickness is nothing to be ashamed of. It is said that nobody is totally immune to motion sickness of some sort, and different motions affect different people. In my own case, the worst is running and rolling down-wind; for my husband it is the bang and crash of beating into wind and sea.

Rich food, too much alcohol and strong odours can set people off. Most people feel queasy at times, and being physically sick is often the end of it. Remember, though, that those unlucky ones who are worse affected and continue to be sick for some hours can rapidly become dehydrated. They then need water, not tea, coffee or any other beverage. It is a good idea also to see that people keep trying to eat something like dry biscuits or bread. I have known people who have continued to feel sick long after they have slept off the effects of seasickness; in fact they were really sick with hunger.

Seasickness has the effect of making people dangerously careless. Thus it affects navigation and other important work, while those who elect to stay on deck in the fresh air must be watched and harnessed for their own safety. Sudden lunges to the rail to be sick over the side are highly dangerous. People should be encouraged to be sick on the narrow sidedecks, which are easily washed down, or in the deck bucket.

Having been sick people quickly become chilled and shivery. There is a tendency for them to fight against going below, sitting instead huddled up in the corner of the cockpit. This may, in part, be a reluctance to 'give in' and a small matter of pride. A wish to be seen doing their share. This is altogether unwise. Far from being of use by staying on deck they are an added responsibility for those on watch duty; it is far better that they turn in, keep warm and try to get some sleep. On the other hand, do not stop people from leaving their bunks if they are beginning to feel better. A spell of steering in the fresh air may be all they need to complete their recovery.

It is quite wrong to say that seasickness 'is all in the mind'. Animals are frequently motion sick. I have known dedicated sailors who are always sick for the first few hours yet they consider it a small price to pay for the many pleasures of sailing. Nowadays I am seldom sick, having found a pill which suits me. If I do feel queasy I simply lie down at once and wait for my body to get used to the motion. It is no foregone conclusion that all beginners are seasick. If you act sensibly the odds are strongly in favour of you not suffering at all. Certainly quiet weather sailing will not affect you and lively sailing is so exhilarating that you will probably forget all about your fears.

There are many travel sickness remedies available, also wrist bands and devices worn behind the ear. Indeed some remedies can be taken in suppository form. For those who are on other forms of medication, or for pregnant mothers, it is wise to seek medical advice, otherwise it is largely a matter of trial and error to see what suits you best. Once you find something which seems to work for you and *have faith in it*, stick to it. My favourite is a drug called *Stugeron* which is basically designed for the relief of Ménière's disease affecting the balance mechanism of the body. It seems to work in over eighty per cent of cases and does not cause drowsiness. Another point in its favour, is that the tablets can be dissolved in the mouth and are tasteless. *Stugeron* is available at most chemists.

Fatigue

Seasickness itself is rarely dangerous. It is the faulty decisions, lowered morale and carelessness which result from it that are dangerous. More insidious is the effect of fatigue which usually accompanies seasickness.

However, sick or not, fatigue is an ever present threat. Our waking/sleeping pattern is turned upside down, and on passage sleep is fragmentary or disturbed. This plus heightened excitement and harder work results in the onset of fatigue at a time usually when the boat is nearing its destination, calling for extra care, good chartwork and clear decisions.

A woman who can take a steering watch, allowing her partner to rest at sea, practically eliminates the problem. Sometimes though, a hard passage, delayed and rough, means that all on board are fatigued often without knowing it, since anxiety keeps tiredness at bay – temporarily. It is then that ridiculous errors creep in, hallucinations become commonplace and lights appear where no lights can be.

If the skipper becomes fatigued the mate should keep an eye on him, and if he cannot be relieved at least a careful watch can be kept over his actions.

2 BOAT BUYING

A woman, totally inexperienced though she may be, will nevertheless use her influence at the earliest stages – the actual buying of the boat. Nowadays yacht builders realize that the woman's influence in the choice of the boat is something which must be considered seriously.

For most couples buying a boat is a substantial investment, possibly involving a marine mortgage and therefore concerning them both deeply. Obviously there will be a price ceiling. If the choice is a new boat the overall ceiling must also include a great many extras: instruments, additional sails, safety equipment and so on, as well as all the personal gear.

Together you must decide whether you want a small boat suitable for the odd night sleeping aboard or a boat capable of being used as a floating home, albeit

The Sadler 26, an excellent family cruiser which is also fun to sail and a safe seaboat.

a modest one. The first might be in the 22–24 foot length range, the second 26–30 foot or larger and consequently much more expensive – not only initially but in terms of running costs too. This choice is very much a joint decision.

Quite often a couple will start with a small weekender in the smaller range and move up the scale as finances improve and a family comes along, perhaps ending up with a 30–35 foot cruiser which offers plenty of living space for growing children and occasionally their friends. Later in life as children leave home it is not uncommon for couples to revert to a smaller boat again, although having become used to the advantages of bigger boats we tend to move down in size with reluctance. Another advantage of this progression from boat to boat is that provided you choose boats which are easily re-sold, the first ones serve to teach us what we *really* want and what to look for in subsequent boats.

The range of boats available is huge and bewildering to a newcomer. Seek all the advice available (from those qualified to give it). Study the type of craft popular in the area you choose as your base. A shallow water area with lots of shallow creeks to explore calls for a boat which does not draw much water. A fine boat which needs six feet of water just to float in may sail like a witch at sea, but she will not be much use for creek pottering.

You will have to decide whether a plump little cruiser with lots of living space below but with an indifferent sailing performance, is preferred to a less roomy boat of the same length but which is more fun to sail. As a cruising mate you should involve yourself in these decisions and maybe reach a compromise. Talk to other sailing people and find out the snags and assets.

Whether you buy new or secondhand is another matter to decide. A secondhand boat in good condition and with a good inventory *should* mean that apart from personal gear and a few improvements of your own choice the boat will be complete and ready to cruise, whereas a new boat may need a lot of extra money spent on her. Always check the manufacturer's inventory lists to see just what is included in the equipment. If you vote for a secondhand boat then note the following advice carefully.

No matter how good the boat may look or how much equipment is included in the asking price you must have a proper marine *survey* carried out on her before buying. Such a survey by a reputable qualified surveyor will list every defect he can find. It may cost in excess of £100 in fees, but more often than not, should you decide to proceed with the sale, the original asking price can be lowered in the light of the surveyor's findings. If the owner will not agree to this then you are better off without the boat.

And be wary of bargains. Just as in the car market, there are many so called boat bargains that can develop into a bottomless pit for your finances.

If it so happens that you are both fairly new to the game and consequently not at all sure what class of boat to buy, there is a great deal to be said for asking a yacht broker to recommend a boat which is within your price range, roughly suitable for your sort of sailing and above all of a class which is popular and in general demand. Thus you can have a couple of seasons in her finding out what you really want and then sell her, probably at much the same price you originally paid for her.

It is very important for both partners to be involved in choosing the boat. Having weighed up the pros and cons of one boat against another much useful knowledge will already have been gained.

Those high-cost extras

Equipment manufacturers make it tempting to spend a lot of money. There are hot-water heating systems feeding electric pumps, various types of refrigerators, hot-air blower systems and even microwave ovens available for small

The Rival 36 is a go-anywhere cruiser and equally at home in mid-Atlantic as she is pottering around the coast. Note the small windows, typical of the long distance sailer, plus the third deep row of reefs in her mainsail.

boats. Provided you have the battery power to run them all they will contribute to both your comfort and ease of living – but they are not essentials. There are other priorities to consider, not always so attractive. VHF radio keeps a small boat within reach of help should it be needed. Electronic navigation instruments as a back-up for routine navigation tell us exactly where we are on the chart,

A roller headsail and an anchor windlass are costly but valuable extras which relieve a crew of much hard work. A windlass makes it easy for the mate to raise anchor – an otherwise backbreaking job.

another obvious safety factor, and an automatically inflating liferaft is the ultimate means of safeguarding the crew. Strictly speaking these are not essentials either – we can sail without them – but money invested in such extras is invested in peace of mind.

Less pressing in that respect perhaps but offering greater ease for working and living aboard are such items as roller headsails (a roller mainsail too if money allows) and for slightly bigger boats an anchor windlass. Extra battery power to cope with the many electric and electronic aids aboard and extra fresh water tank space will also give greater convenience. The roller headsail can be considered a safety feature since it does away with much work on the foredeck, whilst extra batteries ensure bright navigation lights and accurate instruments. Some hard rationalization is needed to decide what is affordable. Remember that as mates our dominion extends beyond the companionway steps.

Equipment below decks

A new boat will probably arrive complete with galley and cooker, water pumps, perhaps a cold box or ice box, cutlery drawers, toilet and washbasin, bunk mattresses and so forth. It is worth checking whether the builder uses safe foam material in the latter. If not, insist on this right from the first – it is a great safety factor. Check whether any foam used on the deckhead and other linings are 'safe' materials also. If this can be incorporated it is well worthwhile. At the present time not all boatbuilders have gone over to the new safety foam materials.

There remain the pots, pans, crockery, cutlery, sleeping bags, pillows etc., to be provided by the new owner. If the boat is secondhand many of these items will be on the inventory, plus a lot more besides, but whether they are to your taste is another matter.

Choose the most modern and up-to-date equipment available and do not make do with old and battered pans and tatty blankets with the mistaken idea that anything will do afloat.

Good quality non-stick pans are worth their weight in gold on board. Fresh water is usually at a premium at sea so pans that wipe clean should be first priority in the galley. There is the added advantage that food can be practically dry-fried in non-stick frying pans with a minimum of fat to clean up so the major parts of the washing up can be accomplished with paper towels before rinsing in fresh water. Choose unbreakable crockery and stainless steel cutlery. Plates and dishes should be as deep as possible to prevent spillage, and plastic or unbreakable glasses are well worthwhile.

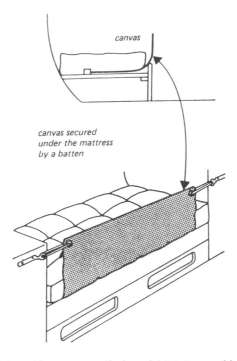

Fig 2 Unless a bunk has side screens or 'leeboards' it is impossible to sleep in it when the boat is heeled and the bunk uphill. Simple screens as shown are adequate and make a useful safe spot for storing things even when day sailing. The strings, or lanyards, serve to tighten the top edge. When not in use they can be tucked under the bunk cushion.

The choice of sleeping bags on the market is enormous, with different weights to suit all conditions. Those covered with nylon or Terylene are ideal; they roll up very neatly and dry rapidly if they get wet. Many boats have Duvets nowadays. Again these stow easily, so personal choice will be the deciding factor. Cushions need careful thought since they usually double as sleeping pillows. Small, lightweight camping pillows are ideal. It is useful to carry stout plastic bags for stowing items like sleeping bags and pillows when they are not required, particularly if the boat is left for any length of time. This way they will stay dry all through the season. Bunk boards or canvases are not items to buy necessarily, but vital if the crew are to sleep easily in a seaway. If none are fitted consider making some. An added refinement, but essential if the boat is to be used by people outside the immediate family, are sleeping bag liners.

Since a large proportion of cruising time is spent in harbour, in marinas, or berthed alongside other yachts, curtains of some sort are essential. Modern yachts are light and airy below, which means large ports and windows and a decided lack of privacy. The best arrangement is to have curtains which fit close against the windows – perhaps on expanded wire top and bottom. A curtain or blind is also useful for the companionway steps when privacy is needed, particularly in marinas or when lying alongside. The added advantage of this is that it will stop draughts to the cooking stove when lying stern to wind.

Lighting is important. Electric lights in the cabin are useful and can often be improved upon by discreet positioning of the various light fittings or replacing centrally placed lamps with fluorescent tubes, which are more economical and effective despite giving off a harsher light. Care and attention to safe stowage of lanterns and all non-electric light is important and a protector must be fitted above lamps if they are suspended from the deckhead to prevent heat and fumes from discolouring it.

Having settled on all the equipment required, there should ideally be ample locker or storage space for stowing it along with all the ship's stores and personal gear needed when cruising. If you are not sure how much storage space you will need, manage as best you can during the first season. It will soon become apparent how much extra space you will need and where it is you need to make it. There is often wasted space in modern fibreglass boats behind interior mouldings which can be adapted, or very large cavernous lockers can be divided into smaller ones.

The Fisher 34 is a motor sailer and thus capable of making fast passages under engine aided by sails, or given a good breeze under sail alone. Well protected from the elements her crew can press on hard in inclement weather without suffering the discomforts of pure sail.

3 LIVING ABOARD

Although the idea of owning a seagoing yacht is to go to sea, the greater part of one's time spent aboard it will be at anchor or berthed alongside. At sea, there are usually some members of the ship's company down below resting whilst the others are in the cockpit enjoying the sailing. In harbour, the centre of activity is often down below, and what seemed to be a spacious cabin suddenly becomes a mass of arms and legs and people moving around getting in each other's way. Boat-people can develop a knack however of occupying a small space which makes it seem larger than it is; the way they move and when they move is all part of this knack and it is worth examining in detail.

In this layout the quarter berth end also provides a seat for the navigator, and a settee berth has its foot tucked under the chart table. Note the thickness of the mattresses, essential as they are laid on a solid base beneath.

First and foremost, the cook has supreme rights when preparing a meal. There must be no shoving past when the cook is at the stove. If anyone wishes to go on deck they should use the forehatch. This is fair and it makes sense if nobody is to be scalded and the cook is to stay sane. The same applies, of course, when serious navigation is in progress. The navigator expects supreme rights when at the chart table, and this is one time when the cook should keep away from the stove, since on many small cruisers the chart table doubles as a working area for the galley.

Of course a great deal depends upon the design as well as on the size of the yacht. The wide beam and high topsides of many contemporary cruisers mean that a galley can be offset clear of the through walkway and the navigation table can be tucked well to port or starboard. The saloon table is often offset with an extra flap used only with a full crowd on board. A typical 30–32 footer, for instance, may also have a large enough forecabin to allow its use as a 'den' for the children to claim as their own.

It takes a while to decide which are the best stowage places; you have to live aboard and sail the boat a few times to arrive at the best arrangement. Having worked out a plan, stick labels on locker fronts – particularly those containing emergency items such as distress flares, safety harnesses etc. Incidentally, never stow life-jackets out of sight. Everyone on board should be allotted one for the course of the sail and be shown where to stow it so that it can be found in the dark if necessary.

Admittedly the above relates mainly to smaller cruisers in the 24–28 foot range where even two people can seem a crowd at times. At 30 foot and above or in beamy, high freeboard hulls freedom of movement below decks becomes significantly easier and much more stowage space is available. However, there is a great deal of difference between what constitutes a five berth boat in the manufacturers' brochures and what is tolerable for civilized comfort. For example we always like to leave one berth free for stowing excess baggage.

The whole matter of living afloat has to be looked at from a marine point of view. A holiday chalet, for instance, may be similar in terms of cubic space but there the similarity ends. A boat may be at anchor so nobody can step off to make room for others aboard. She may offer no shelter from the wind thus everyone crowds below, or she may swing and roll around. On the other hand, in fine hot weather, an anchored yacht becomes something of a lido and swimming pool, hotel and boating lake. Many yachts carry a small sailing dinghy or windsurfer for use in harbour, and when moored in a marina there will be constant coming and going of her crew on shopping and swimming expeditions. Some larger craft may even carry a folding bike.

The concept of a yacht as a holiday base is one thing, but her crew know well

The Prout 'Event 34' cruising catamaran offers much by way of space, comfort and speed. With sleeping berths for six adults plus a spacious deck saloon and the advantage of sailing upright instead of heeling, an owner who has once had a catamaran rarely returns to monohull sailing.

enough that she is also a functional sea-going vessel and that a sudden change in the weather can mean a hurried clearing up and donning of oilskins ready for action. It is a mark of a good crew and a well run cruiser that this can be done in a matter of moments. This change from sybaritic delights to hard practicality also applies to passage at sea. We may start out on a hot lazy day, sunbathing and ghosting or motoring along: an hour later it may be sweaters and oilskins as the yacht, now deeply reefed, plunges into a head sea. Conditions alter all the time, fair weather to foul, in harbour or at anchor, daytime or night-time and most of all between being immobile and being at sea.

The cruiser at sea

The more the boat moves around, pitches and rolls, the less her crew move about. People either sit in the cockpit or lie on their bunks. They are either on watch and sailing the boat or are resting or sleeping. Conversely, the less the boat bobs around the more active her crew becomes. Watches may (or should) be kept so that each person knows when they can take a nap with a clear conscience. When off watch they can potter, fish, sunbathe, read, try their hand at navigating and so on. The layout of the boat below will reflect this.

In even a moderate sea and a modest breeze a cruiser under sail will be heeling over at maybe ten degrees and moving forward with a rocking horse motion combined with a sideways roll. It makes moving around without holding on to something very difficult and anything put down immediately falls over. This is in moderate conditions; if the sea is rough things become hectic. Moving around below is, in any case, likely to induce seasickness so one lies down instead. The navigator tends to keep sessions at the chart table as brief as possible and the cook, unless hardened to it, attempts only the simplest forms of cooking.

The importance of good stowage, now more than at any other time, is vital, particularly of personal belongings and clothing. Usually there are large lockers below the saloon settees, but invariably there will be a sleeper stretched out above them. Try to keep these lockers for general stores not personal belong-ings. Personal lockers are seldom large enough to hold a person's entire seagoing belongings, and if they are stuffed full it becomes a major frustration to find anything without a good deal of rummaging. I prefer to keep frequently used items in my holdall stowed either in my bunk or in the spare bunk. Having to share a bunk with your bag is no hardship, in fact it makes the bunk at sea more comfortable, providing a back rest to stop you from rolling around too much.

A boat must have stout grab rails wherever they can be fixed otherwise it is all too easy to fall and sprain a wrist. In a beamy boat with a wide saloon it is sensible to have a sea-rope stretched tautly fore and aft at about chest height to serve as a grab rail and every bunk should have a lee cloth for the sleeper's security (see Fig 2).

Quite often you will find yachts with an interior that was never designed to be heeled. In particular you will find upper sleeping berths which are unreachable on one tack and untenable on the other. There will be toilet lids that crash down, drawers which shoot out, locker lids which spring open, taps that dribble, settee cushions that will not stay put and many other such annoyances. Not least is the highly dangerous gimballed (pivoted) cooker which fetches up

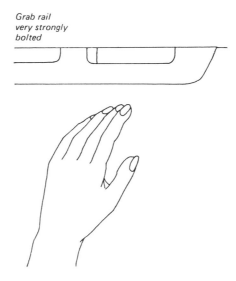

Grab rail
very strongly
bolted

Fig 3 Rough weather bumps and bruises can be avoided if strong grab rails are provided below deck. Certainly the cook will find a rail like this helpful in a seaway.

with a crash because it is unable to swing far enough out. All such short-comings must be found and modified before a yacht is ready for sea.

Bunks and bedding

Sound sleep is as essential as adequate food. When cruising our normal sleep patterns are disrupted especially during night sailing. When cruising it is quite commonplace to arrive at a port at 2 A.M. and leave twenty-four hours later in order to catch the tide. If you are at sea and keeping regular four-hour watches for instance, you will sleep in a series of snatches. Once you are really tired you can sleep anywhere and at any time, but the aim must be to stay well within your fatigue limits. An exhausted person soon can easily make mistakes.

Bunks must be as comfortable as possible. Many boats are equipped with economy thickness settee mattresses, perhaps only three inches thick and laid over a hard surface. Anyone used to a modern bed will find this very spartan. Pillows, too, are often simply small scatter cushions and uncomfortable to use. Sleeping bags that have heavyweight filling are often far too warm for mid-summer and bunks can be either too narrow or too short, or in some cases situated under low lockers which limit movement. While it is not always possible to alter the construction of the boat, quite a lot can be done to make bunks more comfortable.

The accommodation of this Rival 36 is light and airy yet warm with the soft glow of teak panelling. The galley is left foreground and on the right is the chart table. Sleeping berths can be rigged by slotting long bars into notched rests port and starboard.

Four-inch thick foam is about the minimum for comfort. However, two-inch foam underlay can be used under thinner mattresses, secured with tapes or velcro if necessary. Canvas side screens for comfort and security when sailing should also prevent the extra mattress from sliding off. Best of all, if possible, is a criss-cross lattice of rubber upholstery webbing to support the mattress, but in some cases this means cutting away large areas of the fibreglass bunk structure which is not practicable.

4 IN THE GALLEY

Just as the ship's gear will only stand up to the rigours and strains of hard weather if it is properly maintained, so will the crew only keep going at their peak if they are well looked after. It is the cook's job to see that the crew are well fed on board and that when the opportunity for rest comes sleep is undisturbed.

The effects of seasickness apart, fatigue is most often due to insufficient sleep, or inability to sleep. When cruising there is a great deal which can be done to keep the vessel orderly and reasonably quiet below to give those trying to sleep a fair chance of catching up on much needed rest. All equipment and gear should be stowed safely so that it does not scull around as the ship heels or lurches, and annoying rattles and squeaks should be silenced as far as possible by wedging with cloth, foam or paper tissues. In addition the cook should plan the catering to ensure that there is no need to delve into the bilge or forage in lockers, especially at night.

As well as sleep, regular feeding is vital; food gives the body not only energy, but warmth too. It is all the more unfortunate that just as the going gets rougher and the crew is subjected to periods of intense activity, the preparation of food becomes increasingly difficult and the temptation to leave it until conditions improve is greater: this is fatal. Obviously conditions will improve eventually, but long before that the lack of food will begin to have its effect. Gradually the crew will feel exhausted, cold, hungry and tired, and their efficiency will deteriorate considerably. Sickness may take over and it may already be too late to stoke up body heat and energy again.

At this point beware of resorting to alcohol. That spirits are an excellent medicine for those who are wet, cold and exhausted is well known; not so well known is the fact that this applies only if they can rest and keep warm. Indeed, in the days of sailing ships a tot all round was given to any of the crew who had been making intense efforts during a storm, but – and it is a big but – only if they were going below to keep warm.

A tot of rum, whisky, or whatever, gives a quick deep glow of warmth which stays to comfort the body so long as it is warm, but on deck in cold wet

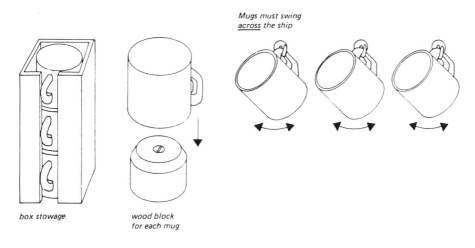

box stowage   wood block
                     for each mug

Fig 4 Mugs stowed on hooks must not swing off as the ship heels. A box with a slot for handles is a good method of stowage, or wooden blocks, one for each mug, can be screwed down.

conditions the effect quickly wears off, leaving the crew weaker and colder than before. This being so, many owners keep spirits tucked away for emergency only, or for when the ship is safely at rest after a hard passage.

During a passage food of some sort – chocolate, nuts, biscuits, fruit, cheese and cold drinks – must be available if producing anything more complicated is out of the question. In fact, what is needed is a selection of high protein foods to help replenish waning energy.

This, of course, is looking on the blackest side and assumes that the cook has not already prepared a meal (hot drinks, stew, soup etc.) in readiness for such conditions. Remember that what may start off as a gentle afternoon sail can become an all-night vigil – such are the delights of sailing! However, a ship's cook who has thought ahead will not be caught out. Ideally the boat will never go to sea for an afternoon sail, a day hop, or an overnight sortie without enough spare food on board to keep the crew going for twenty-four hours if the need should arise.

Planning below

In point of fact the times are rare when cooking of some sort is impossible. A well-planned galley with equipment handily stowed and the stove well gimballed, eases the cook's problems enormously. Storage of crockery is obviously important. Do the mugs stack neatly or are they liable to come skimming off their hooks in a bumpy sea? If it is not possible to stow plates and dishes quickly without juggling them there is obviously something wrong. It should also be possible to take food out of lockers on either tack without packets and tins cascading out. A quiet ship below is something to aim for. Always have strips of foam rubber handy to wedge against plates, dishes, tins, pans etc., that clatter and bang as the ship moves. If there is no sink on board which can be used for steadying mugs in for filling, invest in a deep plastic box, tray or bowl which will serve the same purpose. Incidentally, on the subject of mugs, it is a sensible idea to have some specially deep ones for use in the cockpit when the going is rough.

I always find a few minutes looking around the galley on other cruisers well worthwhile. Designers and interior planners have come up with some excellent and novel ideas for stowage, lockers, work tables, sinks and cooking compartments, and the modern small cruiser is a very workmanlike and practical proposition. Whether you own a modern cruiser or an old craft with accommodation planned in a more traditional style, it is always worth keeping an eye open for new ideas in galley equipment, stowage, and improvements, however small, which make the galley cook's life run more smoothly.

'Putting down' space in the galley is usually at a premium. If it really is short consider a pull-out or folding flap table. Neither need take up much room when not in use, but it could provide just the extra space needed at dishing-up time. Make certain that locker space is used to its best advantage. If lockers are very deep try a divider across them – the back portion can be kept for less used items. Or consider an extra shelf in high lockers.

If the cook is not already provided with a seat or rail for support without using her hands, see if it is possible to include a handhold above the stove and battens on the floor to give a firm foothold. They are very worthwhile additions even on a weekend cruiser. A belt or strap support which leaves both hands free is ideal, especially if more ambitious cruises are planned.

Fig 5 A sliding table under the cooker is sometimes possible and very useful if the galley is small and 'putting down' space is limited.

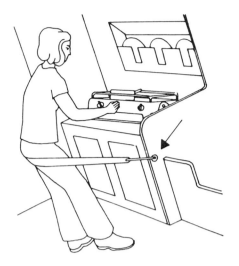

Fig 6 A belt arrangement leaves the cook with both hands free. This must be strong enough to take the whole body weight when the boat heels.

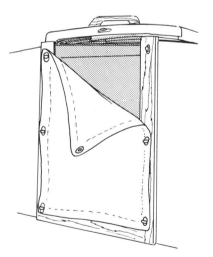

Fig 7 A companionway dodger secured by turnbuckles gives privacy in a marina and protection against draughts when the yacht is lying stern to wind.

It is usually possible to arrange a good current of air below so that the cook can tackle tasks in comfort. However, just occasionally the boat lies to the tide with the wind right aft and if the stove is situated in the companionway the draught can become a problem. A companionway dodger will overcome this to a large extent.

Everyone on board should understand the purpose of the seacocks for the sink and lavatory. All seacocks are turned off between each cruise; some owners turn the toilet seacock off each time it is used, others never when the ship is being lived in. Really it depends on the type of toilet. If the top of the bowl is below the waterline seacocks should be shut off when the boat is left with no one on board, and if there is no vented loop on the discharge line its cock should be closed when under sail. In most cases the sink seacock is turned off when the ship is sailing hard and when she is left unattended.

Water supplies are important, and if life on board is to run smoothly they must be used sensibly and with care. Half a gallon of water per person per day is the absolute minimum for drinking, tea-making etc., but this allows nothing for washing, cooking or washing-up, so reckon on at least two gallons per person as the minimum. Do not be misled, though, by what you read about ocean-crossing yachtsmen and their water ration. You will probably be able to fill your water containers every day or so, so why deny yourself one of life's basic necessities? Each yacht should carry a length of hose and a universal tap fitting, particularly when visiting harbours and marinas since it is often impossible to obtain water without your own hose.

About stoves

How is the stove fixed? Ideally for cooking in a seaway it should swing athwartships in gimbals, i.e., suspended so that its base does not come into contact with the side of the boat as it swings out, or project beyond the edge of its shelf as it swings towards the centre. If the stove should touch the side of the boat, the sudden jerk as the swing is interrupted may be enough to throw pans off, and if it should swing too far in the other direction it may be knocked by the cook with the same result. The alternative is for the cooker to be fixed but provided with rails or 'fiddles' to keep the pans from sliding off. The assumption is that the very minimum of cooking will be attempted in conditions which merit a gimballed cooker. Hot drinks, soup and the warming up of pre-cooked stews etc., can be coped with reasonably well in any but the worst conditions, or when life below is too hectic for cooking anyway. More often than not, only when at anchor or in port will the full-scale meal be attempted.

The type of stove on board will probably depend on what was originally fitted in the case of a secondhand boat, or on the owner's choice in a new boat. It may be bottled gas or it may be paraffin. Both types have their advantages, just as both have their drawbacks. With gas stoves there is a risk of explosion if, through carelessness, leaked gas has collected in the bilge. The paraffin stove is

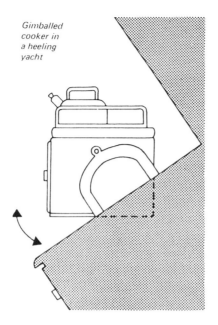

Gimballed
cooker in
a heeling
yacht

Fig 8 A gimballed stove stays level no matter how steeply the yacht heels. Provided nothing stops the swing and no one jerks the stove the pans will stay secure.

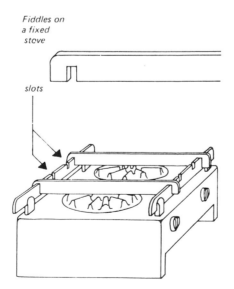

Fiddles on
a fixed
stove

slots

Fig 9 A fixed stove can be fitted with adjustable fiddles (one type is illustrated). While fiddles hold a pan steady they cannot stop spillage from the pan itself.

inclined to be messy, smelly and troublesome, and although non-explosive, is liable to flare-ups.

The paraffin stove takes longer to light and get going than the gas stove, which loads the score heavily in favour of the latter on the small cruiser where, more often than not, the stove is only needed for quick brew-ups, reheating soups and stews, and for quick meals. Personal choice and the type of cruising envisaged will determine which type of stove is chosen, but the following points are worth bearing in mind. Obviously with use the problems of paraffin stoves can be minimized and the risk of explosion with gas stoves are more or less eliminated so long as strict care is exercised.

If gas is the choice the gas cylinder itself should be stowed on deck if possible, or in a gas-tight cockpit locker with a drain. This means that if there should be a leak of gas from the cylinder it will be well clear of the bilges. Any leaks below will therefore be from the stove itself, and careful installation and maintenance of the joints precludes trouble there. The rest is up to the cook.

Here are the points to watch when using gas stoves afloat. The match must always be lighted before the gas taps are turned on: the flame should never be turned so low that it can blow out, allowing gas to escape; and careful watch

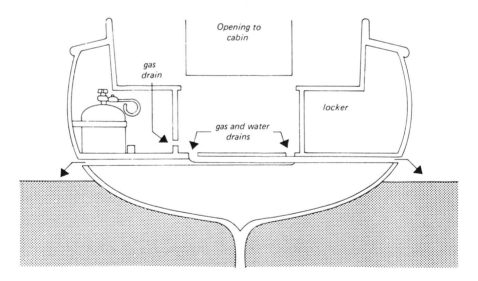

Fig 10 Gas bottle stowage. The crossed drains to the cockpit ensure that water cannot run back into the cockpit when the boat is heeling. Some boats have the drains passing out through the stern instead. The gas bottle in its gas-tight locker has a drain hole which allows any gas leak to escape via the cockpit drain pipes, but other gas lockers may have independent drains which run straight out through the yacht's side.

must be kept on draughts in case they should blow the flame out. Never allow pots and pans to boil over as this could douse the flame. Between use always turn off the gas at the bottle, allowing any gas remaining in the pipes to burn out before turning off the stove taps. (And, incidentally, check each time that the taps *are off* before turning on the bottle again.) The habit of turning off the gas at the bottle each time is a safeguard against children fiddling with the knobs of the stove, as they are prone to do. Most cruisers with bottled gas stoves carry a spare bottle, and replacements are available at most marinas, boatyards and chandlers.

There is a particular risk when the stove is the type which carries its supply cylinder screwed to the base to act as a counter-weight. These cannot be turned off at the bottle. Moreover, quite a lot of gas is discharged into the boat whenever the cylinder is changed.

In countries other than the UK spirit stoves are available, again safe with proper care and very efficient. Gas, though, is on a par with mains voltage electricity ashore – a valuable servant but a terrible enemy if misused. The cook's nose is the first line of defence and my own is super sensitive to the unmistakable odour of butane gas. An electronic 'sniffer' installed in the bilges which sets off a loud squeal if there is any of this heavier-than-air gas present should be considered almost an essential extra.

With careful use galley stoves can have long, worry free lives. However, just in case of emergencies with them, or with any form of paraffin lamps, make sure there is a fire extinguisher handy to the galley and make sure everyone knows how to use it. The extinguisher should be placed so that it can be grabbed from the cockpit if need be. If this is not possible fit an additional extinguisher in the cockpit itself. (See Chapter 9.)

Most modern cruisers have a collapsible pramhood over the main companionway. Whilst this is a boon when the boat is lying head to wind it becomes a huge wind-scoop when the stern is facing the wind as often happens when wind and tide oppose – strong gusts could extinguish a cooker flame. The great advantage though of the pramhood is that it usually allows plenty of fresh air below even in wet weather.

Heating stoves

Few small yachts have permanently installed heating stoves; most use the cooker to warm the cabin on a chilly evening, some have paraffin heaters or gas fires but few have a safe chimney ventilator. This lack constitutes a great risk. Any flame burner gives off gases, burns oxygen and expels water vapour. If these gases are not removed at source the cabin becomes warm, stuffy and deadly. Cases of whole crews dying of asphyxiation are on record.

If there is no chimney there must be constant through ventilation. Open ventilators or port holes are not an acceptable answer because the heads of people sitting or lying down are below the air flow, which should be at waist level *at the very least*.

A proper vented stove is the ideal, such as the charcoal burning *Pansy*. Next in acceptability is the catalytic heater, burning either a petroleum fuel or bottled gas. This 'black' heat cannot set fire to anything if the heater falls over and it burns very little oxygen, giving off barely any fumes at all. Most chandlers stock catalytic heaters.

5 HOW A BOAT SAILS
Strictly for beginners

There are several ways of becoming a mate. It can be because you have the experience; because there is only you and the skipper in the crew or because your partner just happens to be a skipper – a Hobson's choice situation. This chapter assumes the latter.

A first sail can be an electrifying experience simply because everything is so totally new. To be the only one on board who is inexperienced may make you feel utterly useless and perhaps more than a little alarmed.

A sailing cruiser consists of deck, cabin and cockpit and it is from the cockpit at the stern that the boat is sailed. There may be sitting space for six or more people if the boat is to be motored along, but as soon as the sails are set the cockpit becomes a working platform. The crew will need room to move around from side to side without getting in the way of the helmsman, and a total beginner will tend to be tucked away in a corner clear of the action.

A small boat never stops moving. Even when berthed in a marina she will rock and heel as people move around, and once out in open water she will drift with the wind or be carried along by the current unless she is given forward motion by engine or sails so that she can be steered. Perhaps she will be motored out into the middle of a river or harbour and turned head to wind so that the sails can be hoisted.

In even a moderate breeze there will be an alarming racket of flapping sails and rapping ropes. The large mainsail overhead jerks to and fro; forward the second sail thrashes around; then the engine stops, ropes are hauled in and suddenly – sickeningly for the more nervous – the whole boat heels over on her side as if about to capsize and she begins to forge ahead, sails now silent and pulling hard.

Thereafter comes a succession of new sensations. Sometimes the yacht is heeled hard over, plunging along with spray flying from the bows. At other times, and heeling less, she flies along with the sails eased off, and at others she will be upright, rolling from side to side with sails spread like wings and the wind from astern seeming much lighter. There will be occasions when the boat spins round, jerking upright and then heeling again while the crew work with frantic energy to control the ropes (called sheets) and yet other occasions when there is a warning cry of 'gybe-O' and the great sail slams across the cockpit with terrific force. A normal sail to some, a shock to others, at least until the theory of sailing has been grasped.

Sailing simplified

Almost anything can be made to sail before the wind; it will blow along like a paper bag, but a paper bag cannot sail *across* the wind and it certainly cannot be made to sail *against* the wind. To do this we need shaped sails and a boat with a keel that stops her from drifting sideways.

Look at Fig 11 diagram A of a matchbox with a rudimentary square sail. If it had a rudder to steer it we could make it sail dead before the wind, but lacking a rudder it will simply drift any old how, forwards or sideways but always

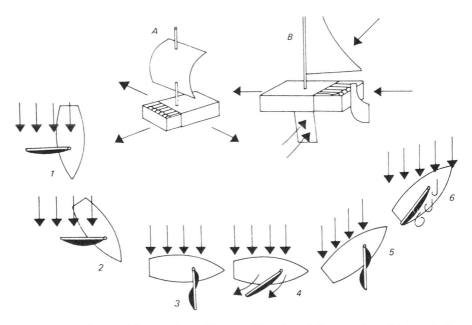

Fig 11 How the wind drives a boat. The matchbox boat (A) can only sail downwind; she will go sideways if the wind blows from the other side. Boat (B) has a keel and a rudder to keep her straight. The keel stops her from being pushed sideways when the wind is from one side. Boats (1) to (6) show how a sail must be gradually pulled in as a boat moves downwind, and then across the wind, and finally close-hauled into the wind.

downwind. In diagram B the matchbox has been fitted with a rudder, as well as a keel to stop it from going sideways and a sail which hinges on its mast so that it can be let out square for going before the wind or let halfway out on one side of the boat or the other for sailing across the wind. How does it do this?

Now look at the series of boat diagrams 1–6. In 1 the boat is running before the wind with its sail fully out. In 2 it is turning a little and the sail has been pulled in slightly but at 3, and still turning, the boat is now broadside to the wind and the sail is flapping uselessly. In 4 the sail is pulled halfway in and the wind is filling it again, causing the boat to forge ahead. By position 5, with the boat still turning, the sail is flapping again – it needs to be pulled in even tighter. In 6 the boat is 'close-hauled' with the sail pulled almost right in but the boat is moving ahead again. Now note that from positions 3–6, with the boat

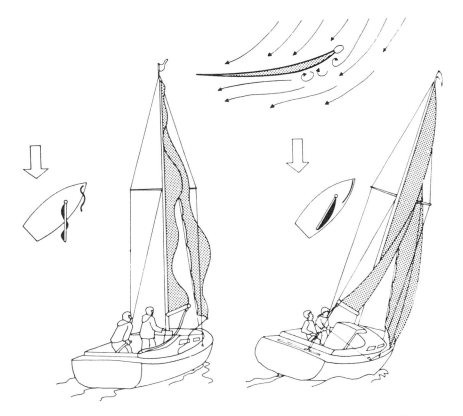

Fig 12 The top diagram shows how wind currents pass either side of a close-hauled sail, eddying behind it and creating a low pressure 'lift' area. An aeroplane wing acts in the same way except that it is driven forwards to create wind, whereas the boat's 'wing' is upright and the natural wind moves past it creating forward drive. The two yachts shown demonstrate a flapping sail which lacks drive and a correctly trimmed sail close-hauled.

broadside to the wind force, it would be pushed sideways were it not for the keel protruding below the boat as in matchbox B.

A keel makes it easier for a boat to go forward than to go sideways. What may be more difficult to understand is how wind, striking a sail sideways rather than merely pushing from behind, can make a boat go forwards. Here we could begin to get into complicated aerodynamics. Suffice to say that it is the same principle as an aeroplane wing. The flow of air under and over the wing provides lift for a plane in the same way that a sail, which is a vertical wing, provides forward drive when the wind strikes it at an angle (Fig 12).

A boat cannot be made to sail dead into the wind because the sail would then merely flap like a flag. Instead she sails as close an angle to the direction of the wind as her design will allow, and in order to reach her up-wind destination she must proceed in a series of zig-zags, tacking or beating as it is called.

This constant adjusting of the angle of the sail is called sail trimming and there is much more sophistication to it than my simple explanation suggests. Basically, though, if the sail of a close-hauled boat is too slack the sail shivers and loses drive. If it is much too tightly trimmed in the advantageous angle is reduced and drive is lost. The same goes for the course being steered, if the helmsman does not point the boat high enough into the wind the boat does not make much ground to windward, while if he points too high ('pinches' the boat) drive is lost and speed falls. All the above will become plain when sailing and can be clearly demonstrated.

Sailing before the wind is not quite as simple as I may have suggested. Look at Fig 13. Here we see a boat running before the wind with her sail let out to one

Wind

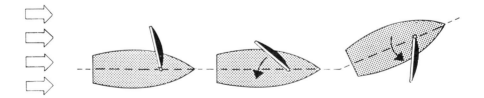

Fig 13 A gybing sail is like a door which slams as the wind gets behind it. To gybe under control the boat is sailed straight while the sail is hauled in; she is then turned a little to bring the wind round to the other side of the sail, and as the boat gybes the sheet is paid out smoothly around a cleat to reduce the shock. A gybe 'all standing' from full out one side to full out the other is safe if intended, but the sheet could catch someone round the neck, or the boom could catch the backstay (or someone's head) when the gybe is uncontrolled.

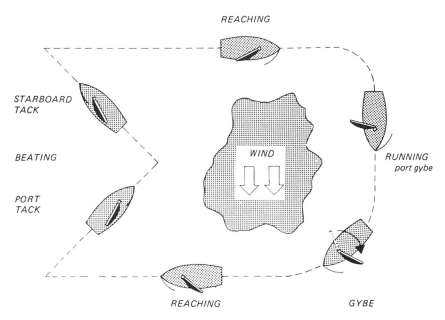

Fig 14 Points of sailing. These are the main points, but many variants of them are used and sails are trimmed in or let out accordingly. The reaches shown are 'broad' reaches, but there are also close reaches (heading up into the wind a little more) and quartering reaches (with the wind a little further aft). If the beating boat were pointed any closer to the wind than this she would be 'pinching'.

side. It may become necessary to steer the boat round a bend in a channel perhaps, and the next diagram shows the sail being pulled in tighter prior to turning. Finally the boat turns and the wind soon gets round the back of the sail and slams it across the boat to the opposite side. This is known as *gybing* and by pulling the sail in a little prior to it happening much of the force of the slamming sail is reduced. A gybe is much the same as a door slamming. If the wind gets behind a half open door it slams either open or shut with some force, depending on the strength of the wind. A sail which is hinged to the mast acts in the same way.

In Fig 14 we see all the 'points' of sailing illustrated. A boat 'reaches' from left to right at the top of the diagram, then 'runs' on port gybe (because the wind is hitting her port side), turns and 'gybes' on to a reach across the bottom of the diagram, finally turning head-to-wind and round until the wind is on her port bow. She is now 'close-hauled' on port tack until she zig zags, 'beating' or 'tacking' to windward on to the starboard tack. These are the main points of sailing. Between these angles there are variants. You can be on a close reach or a broad reach, a quartering or a dead run, a close fetch or hard on the wind.

Learning to sail is like learning to drive or ride a bike; there is a period when it all seems hard work, then suddenly feet find pedals, hands automatically make movements and you have mastered it. In sailing, though, it may be different each time you go out because the wind strength and direction, always altering, make it so.

The wind

It is often only when people begin sailing that they notice the enormous variety of wind both in strength and in character. We will not go deeply into meteorology since that is a vast subject, but it is as well to note a few points in passing.

No wind is constant in speed. It blows in gusts which rise and fall. Neither is it constant in direction; it is continually shifting. This means that while we are sailing, and in particular when sailing close-hauled, the sails are either full or just fluttering and we must steer the boat so that they stay at their proper angle, bearing away and luffing up as required. In the heavy gusts we can also luff up a little as there will be an accompanying shift of direction but in light airs we must steer by feel as well as by watching the burgee at the masthead.

As the wind blows over the water it will average a particular speed of, say, 10 mph. If the boat is moving forward under engine and dead into the wind at a speed of perhaps 5 mph, the wind we feel on our face is one of 15 mph. This is known as the 'apparent' wind as opposed to the 'true' wind; if we are sailing at

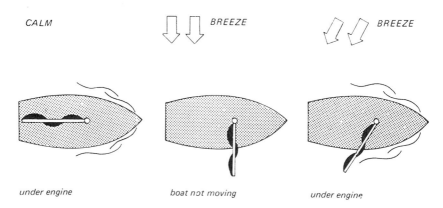

Fig 15 Apparent wind. In a calm a boat under engine makes her own wind; likewise a drifting boat, not moving forward, is subject to the true wind. If she starts her engine and moves forward (or if she trims her sails and begins sailing) the true wind combined with the wind of her forward motion produces a combined effect known as apparent wind.

an angle to the wind, the apparent wind which we feel will have been bent by our forward progress as well as being increased by it (Fig 15). This sounds very technical perhaps, but it makes sense at sea. It also explains why even a light breeze and hot sunshine ashore become rather a chilly business at sea. To add further to this complex problem we can mention the effect of the tidal current which, when it is with us, is actually increasing our speed in relation to the true wind. This accounts for many a rough passage on what should have been a hot and balmy day with just a nice little sailing breeze. One's speed, plus a fair tide, plus the true wind can all add up to 'half a gale', or so it seems.

Winds must be studied, shipping forecasts listened to and signs in the sky heeded at all times when sailing. Wind can make or mar a cruise. Too much and the passage becomes a trial of strength for the crew; too little and – apart from a restful and maybe sun-blessed holiday – time will be wasted under engine or just drifting. And whilst on the subject of weather forecasts, it is a good idea to study them for a day or two before going afloat to get some idea of how the weather pattern is developing.

Some people are purists about sailing, preferring to drift becalmed until a breeze comes up, which it does usually in an hour or so. Others take the view that sails and engine, used separately or in tandem, are one and the same thing – a means of keeping the boat moving forward. I think the sensible approach is dictated by whatever is at stake. If lying becalmed means spending an unnecessary extra night at sea, if the weather is deteriorating, or if people are tired and just want to get in to port, I see no point in not making use of the engine. Likewise, if the quickest way to get into shelter is under mainsail and engine, then this is the most seamanlike thing to do.

6 CREWING
Basics for first-timers

If the cruiser is lying alongside a jetty the correct way to get aboard is at the point where the wire rigging joins the deck near the mast. Do not pull yourself up by the wire hand rails (called guardrails) because these are for emergencies only and should never be strained unnecessarily. The wire rigging, on the other hand, cannot be strained simply by the action of you pulling yourself up. It is quite possible that a trip in a dinghy is needed to reach the yacht. It may be an inflatable or a conventional wood or glassfibre dinghy; in either case it will probably look very small and while it will be safe enough there is a code of behaviour to be observed. Ideally someone should get aboard first then sit down and hold the dinghy close alongside the jetty while you get in. The best way is to extend one foot to the middle of the dinghy floorboards whilst facing the jetty and kneeling on the other leg, then transfer your weight to the seat allocated. Never stand upright, and aim to keep your weight towards the middle of the boat. This may sound alarming, but in practice it is easy. Sit down at once and, unless told otherwise, sit dead in the centre of the seat. The intention is to keep the boat level in the water especially if she is to be rowed. A listing dinghy is much more difficult to row. Do not grip the side of the dinghy; fingers are vulnerable to scrapes if the boat is alongside something else.

On arrival at the yacht others will hold the dinghy firmly against her topsides while you climb aboard. This might be by means of a short ladder rigged for the purpose or may be a matter of clambering aboard by getting one knee on the edge of the deck and hauling yourself up by the rigging using the shrouds, not the guardrails. Do not move from the dinghy until told to do so; do not stand on the edge of the dinghy (the gunwhale) and do not push off with your foot as you climb aboard. It is all quite safe and quite easy. As you gain experience you will learn that it is the crew's job to climb aboard first taking the dinghy painter (the bow rope) and securing in to the guardrail some way forward – so that the dinghy will ride quietly to it without jerking or dropping back.

Even the totally inexperienced crew can start being useful on board right from the start. For instance there will be the mainsail cover to remove; the lacings, toggles or various other fastenings will be obvious. Roll up the mainsail cover starting from aft so that it will be easier to replace at the end of the day and ask where to stow it below. Never leave any unattached item of equipment on deck or it will almost certainly vanish over the side as soon as the wind begins to blow and the yacht starts heeling.

Steering

At the earliest opportunity a beginner must learn to steer. Having someone to steer the boat leaves the skipper free to do other things. If the yacht has a steering wheel there is really no mystery about it apart from the fact that a yacht does not turn quite like a car; it is her stern that moves from side to side as the wheel is turned, but the effect is the same. The bows point the same way as the wheel is turned. Remember also that, unlike a car, a boat does not turn as positively; there is a brief initial delay as the rudder takes effect.

The tiller is totally opposite. The tiller pushed left means bows swinging right and vice versa. Having been given the tiller for the first time do not just stand gripping it rigidly, move it a little to see what happens. You may steer an erratic course at first but the penny soon drops and in the space of a few minutes you

Everybody in the crew should learn to steer, either steering for some visible object, steering by compass or later steering by the wind. It is one of the fundamental jobs of cruising.

will learn the knack. Later, when you have learned to sail, you will find that everything is related to wind direction and you will think of the tiller as being either 'up' or 'down'; i.e., pulled towards the wind or pushed away from it. Moreover the tiller will have a life of its own, but more about this later.

It may also be that the beginner's first attempt at steering will be to keep a compass course. Again, this is no more than a knack to acquire. The compass 'card' can be the traditional flat card marked off in compass points and degrees around its periphery, it can be dome-shaped, or it can take the form of a small window in which the degrees of heading appear. Suffice to say at this early stage that steering the boat means keeping one mark in line with another. The 'card' remains stationary, being aligned with magnetic forces, whilst the boat swings around it. Thus the compass box has a fixed mark or 'lubber line' and the figures on the card move to and fro behind it. As the tiller is moved to the right or left the figures respond accordingly and the trick is to use the tiller to 'push' the figures into line. In actual practice no compass course is ever dead on; it is an average course, a gentle swerving line that swings either side of the heading given.

Steering to a compass does not mean staring hypnotically at the instrument. The eye is more likely to be on some point on a distant headland beyond the bows, or perhaps at a star or cloud – anything that is a useful reference point and, although moving, gives a sense of direction. It is only necessary to glance at the compass every now and then to check on the course.

Dealing with fenders

Although a boat's topsides – the exposed area above the water – are well protected from the ravages of salt and climate they are very vulnerable to dents, scratches and abrasions which means that when the boat is brought alongside another boat, jetty or wall some padding is needed. This takes the form of inflated plastic sausages which can be dangled over the side, and it is the crew's job to position these when needed and to take them in again afterwards.

These fenders (they used to be called 'fend offs') are usually stowed in one of the large cockpit seat lockers, and since getting them out often means disturbing the skipper or helmsman it is best to do this well in advance, not just as the boat is approaching the dock and tricky steering is involved.

A beginner to the job will be told exactly where to position the fenders – spaced out along the topsides where the boat is widest and maybe one towards the stern and another forward of the mast. The aim is to suspend them by their rope tails from the guardrail wires, not dragging in the water but not too high either. Much depends upon the wall, the jetty height, or height of topsides if going alongside another yacht. On a small boat, having tied them to the guardrail in preparation they are often lifted and laid along the deck until they are needed because it is not considered to be good seamanship to go around with them dangling over the side.

The most important thing of all is to ensure that the fenders are tied securely but in such a way that they can be untied quickly should they have to be shifted elsewhere in a hurry. Either a clove hitch or a round turn two half hitches must be used (see Fig 32). Since these two knots have a dozen other uses aboard a boat, it makes sense to learn them right from the start and to practise until you can tie them quickly and without having to think about it.

Steering, dealing with fenders and handling the jib sheets are really the first skills for a beginner crew, plus a few other jobs as they come along. Working sheet winches will be dealt with in succeeding pages.

Mooring buoys

Once a mooring buoy is let go the boat is free to move and must be given forward power from motor or sails so that she can be steered. Thus it is easy to see that if the buoy is let go too soon the boat may drift straight into another one moored nearby before she can be got under control. Accordingly the mooring must never be let go until the order is given. Never anticipate this order. Once the mooring buoy has been thrown well clear the crew should call out 'All clear' or something of the sort, so that the helmsman understands clearly.

The mooring is usually rope (or chain) made fast to a strong cleat or post on the foredeck, and the buoy may be on the end of an extra length of line which lies coiled on deck while the boat is moored. Once in the water, the mooring sinks and the buoy marks it so that it can be picked up again. The mooring must be let go from its post and allowed to run smoothly out over the bow fairlead, and finally the buoy and rope must be *seen to be clear* of everything on deck and thrown clear. Sometimes buoy and rope are thrown clear first and chain last, but if this is done be sure to throw them through the same gap in the rails or pulpit that the chain is led through, otherwise the boat will suddenly bring up with a jerk as the buoy tangles around a stanchion (Fig 16). The reason for throwing the buoy clear is that if this is not done, its rope may be caught up by the propeller or, in the case of a twin keeled yacht, around one of her keels.

Alternatively a mooring buoy may be too large to be lifted out of the water; it may support the mooring chain beneath it with the yacht being secured to a large ring on top to which is attached a short length of heavy riding chain.

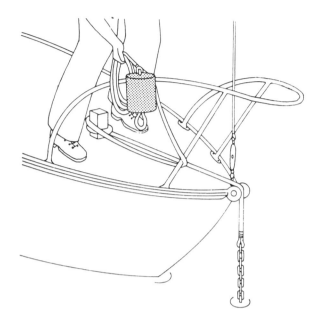

Fig 16 Letting go the mooring. The buoy and its rope have been led forward and out through the gap in the pulpit by which they originally came in. Failure to do this would mean that when the mooring is dropped the buoy rope might be left hitched round a stanchion.

Letting go in this case is a matter of uncleating this chain from the forward cleat and seeing that it drops clear of the bow. Having done this and signalled that it has been let go, the crew stays there to watch the buoy and to point to it for the benefit of whoever is at the helm since they will not be able to see it from the cockpit.

If the boat is to leave her mooring under sail the operation is sometimes different and slightly more complicated. She will probably be lying head to wind on the mooring and it may be important that she goes off on, say, port tack (i.e., with the wind blowing on her port side) so that she has room to gather speed and steerage in a clear space of water between other moored boats. This means that the mooring must not be let go while the boat's bows are pointing in the wrong direction. The helmsman may yell out 'let go' but by the time you have got the chain clear the boat may have swung back and be pointing the wrong way. A moment or two later she may have swung again and be facing the right way and that is the moment when the mooring must be slipped clear. In other words the crew on the foredeck must know what the helmsman intends to do. Usually the jib will be backed momentarily so that it pushes the bow in the right

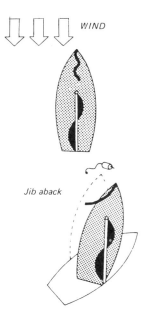

WIND

Jib aback

Fig 17 This diagram shows how a boat's bows are turned in the desired direction by backing the jib just before the mooring is let go.

direction and this impedes work somewhat. The experienced mate will grab the sail and do the backing in an emergency, but more of that later (Fig 17).

Due to lack of room in today's crowded harbours moorings are usually picked up under engine, but sooner or later an engine failure, or more probably rubbish of some sort jamming the propeller, means it will have to be attempted under sail. The skipper will have tried to handle the boat so that the mooring buoy is approached very slowly and right on the nose – but it is not always possible to be successful in this endeavour. The skipper may take a run at it too fast hoping someone can grab it with the boathook, haul it aboard and make it fast *before* the full weight of the yacht comes on it! Or he may misjudge it so that the boat stops dead when it is just out of reach – in which case someone must have telescopic arms!

Standing on the foredeck, a little to one side so that the helmsman can see the buoy, it is possible to sense whether it will be a good shot or a bad one, and to prepare for it. It is sometimes necessary to give directions to the helmsman, who may lose sight of the buoy once it is blacked out by the bows. The best method is simply to point at it. Arm waving this way or that could be misinterpreted as an instruction to push the tiller one way or the other. Pointing leaves nobody in doubt.

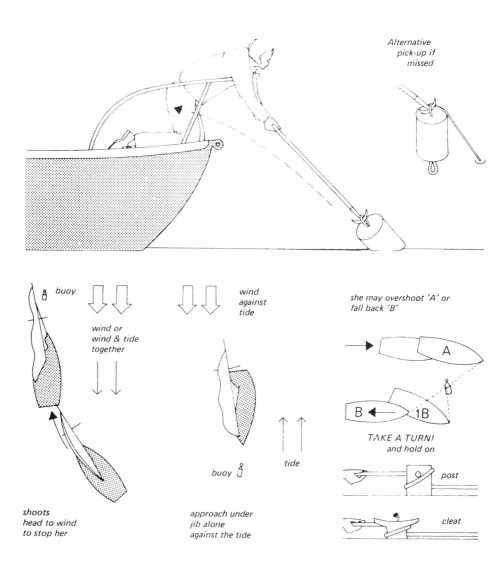

Alternative
pick-up if
missed

buoy

wind
against
tide

wind or
wind & tide
together

she may overshoot 'A' or
fall back 'B'

A

B ← ↑B

TAKE A TURN!
and hold on

tide

post

buoy

cleat

shoots
head to wind
to stop her

approach under
jib alone
against the tide

Fig 18 Hook the buoy as early as possible and get it aboard through the proper gap in the pulpit rails. If the buoy cannot be hooked easily, pick up the rope beneath it (inset). Take a turn round the deck cleat or post with the rope. The lower sketches show how a sailing boat usually shoots head to wind in order to stop as close as possible to the buoy, although with wind and tide against each other she may do as shown in the centre sketch. Sometimes the yacht may approach too fast and overshoot the buoy – all the more reason for taking a turn as soon as you can.

The buoy will have a loop of some sort and into this the hook of the boat-hook must go. If you miss, it is often better to hook the buoy rope itself so that the weight of the now dangling buoy allows you to lift it. Either way, get it on board as fast as you can, especially if the boat is still moving fairly fast. Remember that the buoy must come aboard so that it has a clear run under lifelines etc. (Fig 18).

The aim now is to 'take a turn'. This means that instead of laboriously trying to pull in all the slack and make the chain fast in the full and final manner, enough of the buoy rope is pulled in quickly to wind round the post or cleat two or three times, preferably in a figure of eight manner to hold it temporarily. The end is then held waiting for the strain to come on it as the yacht continues to move forward until she has reached the end of her tether. Then the buoy rope brings her up, stretches taut and takes the strain until she drops back. By this time, or well before, the skipper will have joined you on the foredeck and taken over the rest of the operation to check that all is secure and fast.

If you miss the buoy, do not run aft for another shot at it from the stern, especially when under sail. Even if you got it aboard and were able to hold on, the boat would then be moored in such a way as to cause her to swing stern-to-wind under full sail. The result would be a most horrible pantomime. Do not try to hang on to the buoy at the risk of being pulled over the side. The helmsman's job is to make it possible to get it aboard; if he muffs it and you have done your honest best, it is better to let him sort out his troubles and come round to have another try.

The above may be a little different in the case of one of those large mooring buoys referred to earlier. Unless it has a pick-up line of some sort attached to it a line will somehow have to be passed through the large ring on top, and since it will be out of reach of your hand and arm this poses a problem. Hanging on by means of a boathook is impractical – for obvious reasons. There are, however, special boathooks obtainable which either clip the end of a line to the ring or pass a rope's end through it and back leaving the boat attached by a double line. It remains quite a tricky matter to snare the ring on the buoy with one of these gadgets so do not feel too surprised if you miss it and need several runs at it. There is, however, one other method.

You need a suitable rope attached to a bow cleat and then led outside the rails and everything else including all rigging, right back to amidships, which is where in most boats the decks are lowest. By lying prone at this point, rope's end in hand, it is then the helmsman's job to over-shoot the mooring buoy and bring it bumping gently aft along the yacht's topsides to where you can reach it and either clip on your rope or pass the end through and quickly make a couple of half-hitches.

There are other methods of mooring a yacht such as 'trots' in which boats are

If the mooring buoy is out of reach and lacking a pick-up line, an alternative means of attaching a rope to it is to lie on the side deck where the hull is lowest. A rope has been attached to the bow and led outside the rigging and rails. The helmsman manoeuvres to bring the buoy within reach, the rope is quickly made fast and then hauled in from the bows.

moored between two buoys so that they cannot swing with the tide. This takes up less space and sometimes two or more yachts lie alongside each other. Or instead of buoys there may be large posts with sliding rings to which the bow and stern lines are made fast. In these cases there is usually a long pick-up line running between the buoys or posts, and having hooked it with the boathook and hauled it aboard to a cleat at the bow the skipper can be left to adjust things to his liking. In the absence of such a line it may be possible to go alongside a neighbouring yacht on the same trot and then pass your bow and stern ropes to the posts by moving ahead and astern. Failing this it is better to secure the first line to whichever post or buoy is up-tide or up-wind, and then drift down to reach the other. Mooring in marinas and yacht docks is covered in Chapter 8.

Sail handling

We have taken a fairly close look at the how and why of sailing and the mate's part in crewing, but now we must get still closer to the subject.

Each time a boat tacks or gybes, bringing the wind from one side to the other, the sails have to be trimmed across. In the case of the mainsail it may not need touching unless adjustment is needed to harden it in or let it out a little. When the boat passes through the eye of the wind the mainsail swings across automatically. The jib sheets, however, must be trimmed across. This means that if the boat has the wind blowing on her port side (on port tack), the starboard (or lee) jib sheet is in use and the port (or weather) one is slack. As she tacks, the jib shakes and rattles mightily, the starboard sheet is slacked off and the port one hauled in.

In light breezes this is an easy job soon mastered, but in fresher winds muscle power alone is not enough and so the sheet winches begin to earn their keep. These winches are so designed that they will revolve in one direction only. The

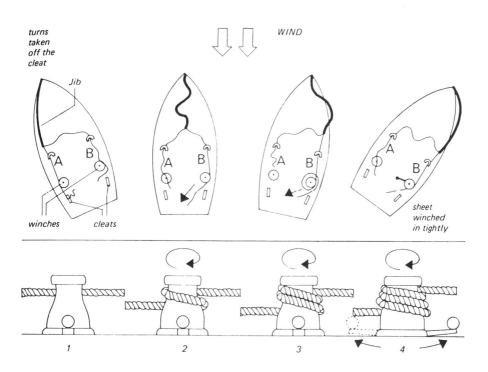

Fig 19 Working the sheet winches. The diagram shows the stages of a boat tacking from starboard to port tack. The sheet to leeward (A) is released as she comes around and the new lee sheet (B) gathered in slowly so that the sail is not backed. A turn is taken around the winch (third sketch) as the jib begins to fill and the slack sheet is spun in as fast as possible. More turns must be put on the winch before the full load of the sail develops and the rest of the slack winched in by means of the handle. The bottom sketches show a winch in action. As soon as there is a load on it the slack end of the rope must be held tightly while winching in or the turns will fail to grip.

sheet is wound round the barrel three or four times, in the direction which allows the winch to revolve as the sheet is pulled in. A lever handle is then used to turn the winch until the sheet is considered tight enough.

There is a knack to it, but it does not take long to master and in mastering it most of the hard work is avoided. Let us sum up by imagining a tack being made. The boat is tramping along close-hauled and the helmsman wants to go about. The correct order is then 'Ready about'; the crew loosens the end of the sheet from the cleat near the leeward winch, but without allowing it to slacken off the winch itself. On the command 'lee-oh' the helmsman puts the tiller across and the crew spins the turns off the winch, takes a quick glance to make sure nothing is liable to snag, and takes hold of the new lee sheet. As the boat comes nose to wind the sheet is pulled in and wound quickly (and in the correct direction) round the winch. As much of the slack as possible is pulled in while the sail is flapping, causing the winch to spin merrily. At the very moment when the sail fills with wind on the new tack the winch handle is used to bring in the last few feet of sheet and harden the sail well in. Finally the end of the sheet is made fast on the cleat without losing any of the hard-won tension in the process (Fig 19).

Most sheet winches are two-speed. This simply means that you can wind the handle in one direction to get the sheet in quickly and as soon as it becomes hard work you reverse the direction and the low gear is engaged, i.e., you turn at the same speed but the winch drum revolves more slowly but with more power. Once it becomes really tough, instead of trying to wind the handle right round in a full circle you can begin to 'ratchet' by moving the handle back and forth in short strokes. Complex though it may sound, it is all quite simple in practice. I should also mention that boon to the short-handed, the self-tailing winch. Ordinarily while the mate is winching in, the person on the helm or another nearby keeps a steady pull on the end of the sheet, without which, of course, the rope will not grip the winch barrel. A self-tailing winch obviates this necessity.

In a boat with a male/female crew, unless the woman is an olympic javelin thrower the choice of sheet winches powerful enough for her to use unaided is very important; a thing to remember when first equipping a new boat.

The mainsheet does not pose much of a problem. It is arranged so that the work is made easy by the use of blocks, and it is usually the helmsman's job to adjust it since he is nearest to it in a small cruiser. However, it is as well to know just what effect the mainsail has on the steering because there are times when the mainsheet needs to be slackened off quickly and hauled in equally fast.

In most small vessels the mainsail tends to make the boat turn up into the eye of the wind and the jib counteracts it. Thus, if it is necessary to make the boat turn quickly *away* from the wind – to bear away, in fact – the mainsheet must be

Sheeting in the jib. The mate's left hand is maintaining a firm pull on the tail of the sheet without which the turns on the winch barrel would slip. She is winding in a clockwise direction, but as soon as the strain becomes too great she will reverse direction and thereby use a lower and more powerful gear.

let out if it was previously trimmed hard in. In a sudden emergency, when the skipper has his hands full and is trying to bear away, a quick-thinking crew would jump for the mainsheet and let it go for him. Our old friend the gybe is another case for smart mainsheet handling.

Running before the wind with the mainsail right out, a gybe (and the consequent crossing of the mainsail from one side to the other) means that, as it swings over, the sheet will be momentarily slack unless it is hauled in smartly and then let out again as the sail swings over. A slack sheet can lassoo the helmsman or foul up on a projection. It also allows the boom to flip and perhaps become hooked against the backstay causing a total loss of control of the boat.

The standard practice in a gybe and with a fresh breeze blowing used to be to 'surge' the mainsheet to relieve the shock, but most yachts now have a jamming device on the lower block of the mainsheet which prohibits doing this. If the sail looks likely to bang over with great force, therefore, we should:
(a) haul in on the mainsheet as tightly as possible while the boat is stern to wind,

(b) flip the jammer free just as the boom crashes over and
(c) let the sheet run free.
Do not grip the sheet tightly in your hands while it is running – you could get
rope burns on your palms.

Setting and stowing sails

In the modern small cruiser there are very few ropes to be handled. We have
already identified sheets, but there are also halliards (haulyards in olden days)
by means of which the sails are raised, and downhauls or tack tackles used for
tensioning sails downwards after they have been hauled up on the halliards and
made fast. Finally there is the topping lift which simply holds up the end of the
boom.

In order to hoist or 'set' a mainsail, the yacht must be more or less head to
wind otherwise the sail will be flattened against the mast by wind pressure and
be impossible to move. Look upwards while pulling on the halliard. The sail will
be flapping vigorously and liable to snarl up on the rigging as it travels up the
groove or track in the mast. If it sticks do not continue hoisting until you have
found *why* it is sticking. Having hoisted as high as your strength will allow the
main halliard winch on the side of the mast or coachroof is used to finish the
hoisting and apply tension. In some cases there may be a downhaul attached to
the bottom of the sail for this purpose, but the aim is to get the luff, or forward
edge of the sail, stretched tight – and the more wind there is the tighter it must
be.

Having made fast the halliard on its cleat beside the winch, coil up the

Fig 20 The end of the halliard should have a knot in it through the cleat (A) to
prevent it from running aloft out of reach. To secure a halliard to a cleat take a round
turn followed by a series of figure-of-eight turns (B). Having secured it, take a doubled
length of halliard, give it a few twists and then hitch the coiled rope to the top of the
cleat (C).

remainder and hang the coil neatly (Fig 20). This is very important. If the boat begins heeling steeply a badly coiled halliard can quite easily get washed over the side and end up by fouling the propeller. It remains only to tighten the 'kicking strop' under the boom, usually a matter of tugging a rope through its jamming block until the strop is really hard. A kicking strop helps make the sail set flatter and holds down the boom; quite important if the sail has to be gybed hurriedly.

Some wife-mates sail for years with their husbands and yet never venture out of the cockpit while sailing. This is largely a matter for mutual agreement. In rough weather a man may feel that he is better able to hang on and wrestle with the sails; that leaving his mate on the helm to nurse the boat along quietly while he works on deck is a safer arrangement. This is arguable – the more the mate, of either sex, can do to become an all-rounder the better. Of course, in the case of a wife-mate who lacks the physical strength to hang on and work at the same time, it is plainly stupid to tackle what may be a dangerous task. It is often a matter of sensible compromise; let her learn to go forward in reasonable weather and let him do the rough stuff – that way both are satisfied. She could cope at a pinch if really necessary (say the skipper had injured a hand and the boat had to be reefed) and no undue risks are taken.

First and foremost comes the matter of safety and the need to exercise great care when moving around on deck (man-overboard will be dealt with later). When going forward do so on the uphill side if the yacht is heeling – and usually she is under sail. There will be knee-high guardrails along the sides of the deck, but it is best to behave as if they were not there at all and keep a firm grip on the grab rails on the coachroof, on the rigging, the mast and so on. It is no bad plan to wear a safety harness at first even in calm weather, and always in rough weather or at night.

It is advisable to sit down to perform whatever task is required. This is the safest of all methods and nobody will laugh at you because it is a mark of the expert – in rough weather certainly. Either sit or kneel, but sit for preference and clip on the harness hook to rail or rigging.

The hoisting procedure is similar for jib or genoa – if lighter winds call for this latter type of jib – except that it may have to be hanked on to the stay. We will not dwell on this operation since it will call for a practical demonstration if it is to be tackled by the crew. However, be sure that no hanks are twisted, that the sail is not snagged around, say, the anchor, that the sheets are clear to run and that the halliard is clipped on; also look aloft to ensure that it is not twisted around the forestay. One word of warning. The sheets may be attached to the sail by means of a patent clip-hook and when the sail is flogging around this hard metal fitting can inflict painful blows or smash glasses – so beware!

The development of the roller headsail has made foredeck work a great deal easier as it is no longer necessary to have to keep changing from one size jib to another. Rather like a roller blind set on end, the roller jib is controlled by a long line led back to the cockpit. When the sail is to be set it is unrolled by pulling on

This crew is removing the winch handle from the halliard winch. Note that he is wearing a safety harness and that the harness line is clipped to a 'jackstay' wire on the deck, which will allow him to move in safety from cockpit to foredeck without having to unclip his line.

either of the sheets and at the same time allowing the line to run free, but with just a little tension on it. Allowing it to run through the palm of the hand is enough; this ensures that the line rolls evenly on the drum of the roller. Similarly, when the sail is rolled up the sheet is eased off while pulling on the line to turn the drum; again a little tension should be kept on the sheet to ensure that the sail rolls evenly. In a fresh breeze the initial pull on the line can be quite heavy, indeed some roller sails have a small winch to operate them. By starting the pull on one of the sheet winches, however, this difficulty can be overcome.

Now and then a sail needs to be set while the yacht is pitching and rolling around at anchor and while the skipper may be occupied with other things. It may also have to be done in the dark and conditions may be such that the mate has to tackle the job alone. Knowing the ropes and the drill is what matters then.

The stowing of sails also calls for skill. The skipper may have his hands full manoeuvring the boat under engine in a tricky spot and may call for the sails to be lowered. It is simple enough to let go the halliards, but not always so simple to get the sails down if they are filled with wind. This means that they must be pulled down by hand and will balloon out and flog. All the time they are ballooning and flogging they are restricting the helmsman's view, so speed at this time is essential. (Here, incidentally, a word of warning – never stand on Terylene sails, they are extremely slippery.) After subduing the sails a tier is used to hold them temporarily. These are usually kept handily at the base of the mast or in the cockpit. The tier is passed around the sail and its boom, or the sail and its stay if it is a jib, and tied with a reef knot (see knots, hitches and bends). The slack of the mainsheet is then taken in to stop the now sail-less boom crashing around.

The feel of the boat

There is a great deal of difference between 'holding the tiller' under strict instructions to push it this way or that and 'taking the helm'. A mate who can take the helm under sail or power and on any particular point of sailing (beating, reaching, running, etc.) and under any conditions of wind and sea, immediately gives the skipper freedom to navigate with care or do other essential jobs. Unless he can be sure that the boat will be sailed safely and properly he will devote only half his mind to what he ought to be doing, and the consequences could be serious if he makes a mistake.

As mentioned earlier, a tiller works in the opposite direction to what one might expect. This apparent paradox makes sense when a boat is under sail and heeling over. We forget about left and right or port and starboard and think in terms of up or down. Imagine the yacht to be heeling and sailing along. You are sitting on the uphill or windward side with the wind blowing on that side. If you pull the tiller towards you it will be coming up, i.e., towards the wind. If you push it away from you it will be going down or away from the wind. Only when a boat is on a dead run before the wind does this ruling cease to apply (Fig 21).

Under sail, beating or reaching or on any point other than a dead run, the 'feel' of the tiller is directly related to the effect of the sails. As we have seen, the force of the mainsail tends to make the boat want to turn her nose up into the wind, and in order to prevent her doing this there is the effect of the jib to balance her. As a boat heels and the wind strengthens, however, she tends to exert more and more of her willpower, so to speak. If the tiller is let go she will

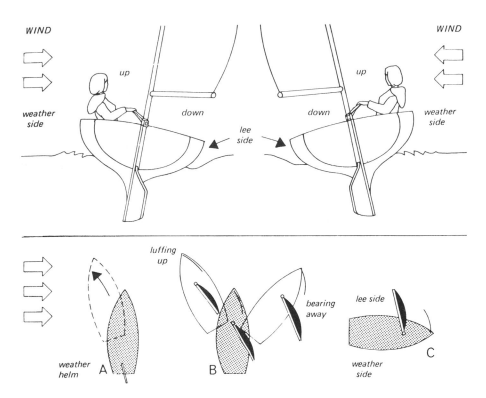

Fig 21 These sketches show how weather side and lee side are unrelated to port and starboard – the 'windy' side is the weather or windward side. In (A) the yacht has a natural tendency to steer herself into the wind and the tiller is kept 'up' (upwind) a little to counteract this. (B) shows the difference between luffing up and bearing away; changes, of course, entirely related to the direction of the wind and irrespective of port or starboard. In (C) the boat is running before the wind, but there is still a lee and a weather side, according to which side the boom is on.

automatically slew round until she is head to wind. Some boats have this tendency to a strong degree and are said to be 'hard headed', others are better balanced due to sails and hull shape and have very little, if any, of this 'weather helm' as it is called. Most family cruisers have it to some degree and it is not really a bad thing. It is easier to get the feel of such boats. When at the tiller you will feel it pulling against you gently. To make the boat turn away from the wind you pull against the pull, and if you want to head up into the wind a little then allow the tiller to have its own way a touch, letting it get away from you or *down* a bit.

As explained earlier, the wind is never quite constant in strength or direction, consequently the helmsman is continuously pulling and easing the tiller to keep the boat on course or to keep the sails full of wind. If sailing close-hauled, for instance, the wind may head a shade so that the jib begins to flutter. Instantly the tiller is pulled *up* and the yacht bears away a few degrees until the sail stops fluttering. Conversely the wind may free just a little so that if you wish you can sail even closer to the wind, therefore pulling the tiller *down* a touch.

Usually a crew that does not yet know how to sail by the wind, as we say, is told to 'steer for that buoy' or whatever the mark may be. Accordingly the bows are pointed at it and the tiller moved to suit. The knack is to use the tiller as little as possible. Wide sweeping movements (which will be made at first) are soon tailored down to the imperceptible give-and-take tiller technique.

Under engine life is less tricky, although a boat with single propeller will also try to wander off course. This is due to the side paddling effect of the propeller, but it is very slight and soon corrected.

The mate on the helm, with skipper working on deck, must be ready for the sudden extra gust of wind which makes the boat heel far over. If this happens luff up slightly, pointing the bows a little nearer to the eye of the wind so that some of the weight of the wind is shed. Alternatively, and if circumstances merit it, the mainsheet can be eased out a few feet so that the wind is spilled from the mainsail. If the skipper is trying to change a sail he will bless the mate who can gentle the boat along without deluging him with spray and making his job more difficult – provided the luffing is not overdone and the boat tacked round altogether.

Many of us have a blind spot where engines are concerned. Engines, we feel, are the skipper's department. However, all mates should be thoroughly familiar with engine starting and stopping procedures and use of throttle and gear, the latter usually one and the same lever in today's yachts. With more experience it is also important to be able to make the basic manoeuvres under engine such as steering quietly up towards a buoy, putting the engine out of gear, ghosting up to the buoy and then perhaps giving a touch of astern gear. In many cases a sailing couple mutually prefer the mate to take the helm when coming alongside a marina berth, leaving the skipper to juggle with the ropes, but this is an individual choice. It is certainly important that the mate should be able to handle the engine when approaching an anchorage. Although the mate may prefer to be forward and letting go the anchor it is far more sensible, certainly in the case of a female, for her to take the helm while the man goes forward. More of this later.

Giving orders – and taking them

The biggest bone of contention aboard a yacht often lies in the orders, vocal and visual, given by the skipper to the person at the helm. It is worth getting this clear right from the start. When he gestures to the right, for instance, does he mean that he wants the bows of the yacht to go that way or does he want the tiller pushed in the direction indicated? Likewise, when he yells 'Port a bit', does he mean bows or tiller? The odds are that he wants the tiller pushed when he gestures and the bows turned when he shouts! Obviously this is something to sort out right from the start. There may be moments when it is not easy to remember which is port or starboard. Remember the *aide-mémoire* 'Jack left port' and that port wine is red. Thus the navigation lights are red to port and green to starboard.

In these early stages of learning to be at home afloat, much is perplexing and even worrying. A small yacht really moves very slowly, probably rarely faster than 8 mph unless she is a fast power cruiser. For all that, even under sail, there is a great deal of noise of rushing water and flapping canvas, and things seem to happen at break-neck speed. Small emergencies – which certainly do not threaten life and limb – crop up out of the blue and a skipper is apt to thrust the tiller, or a rope, into his mate's hands and expect them to cope, somehow.

At such times calmness – or at least the appearance of calm – is essential, because there are few things as contagious as panic. Some skippers, however, seem to take pride in ranting and roaring and later primly apologizing for their explosions, but they are not to be encouraged. A good skipper in a crisis gives orders quietly (no matter how dry his throat may be) and, moreover, he gives them singly. He does not rattle out commands faster than his mate can possibly deal with them. More importantly, a calm mate usually means a calm skipper.

Anchor work

The anchor has been the symbol of hope since early times and it remains, very

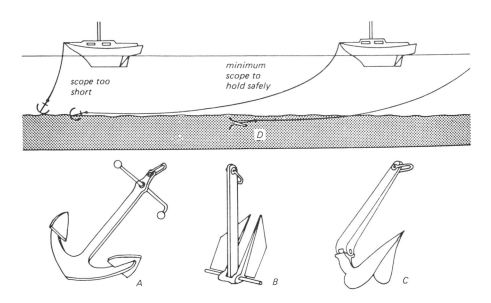

Fig 22 If the scope or length of cable paid out is too short the anchor will fail to bite. The minimum safe scope is three times the depth of water at high water in the anchorage, but more may be needed in strong winds or if the seabed is poor holding ground. The three typical anchors shown are (A) Fisherman, a non-burying type, (B) Danforth or Meon burying anchor, and (C) plough type, also burying. (D) Shows a Danforth at its normal depth in softish sand.

often, the last recourse of the small yacht in a tight spot. An anchor is designed to dig into the seabed and either to continue to dig down the harder the yacht tugs on her cable or to lie with one arm and fluke spiked in firmly. If the strain becomes very great the anchor will either drag, bury deeper, or rise to the surface of the seabed and then dig in and bury again.

This is a great simplification of what happens to both the plough and Danforth type buriers and the surface-holding Fisherman type of anchor. In all cases an anchor depends for its hold upon the type of seabed, the anchor's size and suitability for the boat, and the length of anchor cable paid out. The length of cable needed is from three times the greatest depth of water (tides rise and fall remember) to five times, but never less than three times and more if space to swing on the tide without hitting nearby boats allows. In a real gale and in an exposed anchorage yachts may have to let out eight or more times the depth of water to prevent them dragging (Fig 22).

From this it can be seen that an anchorage must be chosen with care and it is no use complaining if the skipper anchors in a spot which is a long boat row from the landing place ashore. Safety first, convenience second. It is also easy to

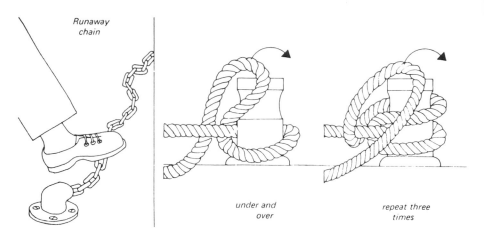

Runaway
chain

under and
over

repeat three
times

Fig 23 If the yacht is anchored in deep water the chain may run out too fast and pile up on top of the anchor in a tangle. Never grab a runaway chain – stamp on it. Rope or chain cable should never be made fast in a way which could tighten and be difficult to let go. The tug-boat hitch shown is the correct way and it is safe and easy to undo, especially with chain.

see that anchors must be let go carefully so that they are not buried under a heap of chain, which might tangle with them and prevent them working properly (Fig 23). While the skipper may have to concentrate on finding the ideal spot where there is room for the yacht to swing as the tide or the wind changes direction, it is often the mate's job to let go the anchor precisely where he wants it. Remember the spot where the anchor goes down is not the position in which the yacht will finally lie; she will end up some way to one side or the other.

We used to measure depth of water and anchor cables in fathoms (six feet) but nowadays charts are based on metres and it is more convenient to think in metres when we are letting the anchor go. What is more important, though, is that the anchor cable, whether rope or chain, is marked in some way so that we know how much we have paid out. Paint marks at five metre intervals may be used, one for five metres, two for ten metres and so on is adequate. Some people simply use one mark at each interval but in red, white, blue etc.

When the order to let go is heard the anchor must be dropped at once and allowed to fall unchecked to the seabed. Having some rough idea of the depth we can avoid letting too much cable out in one rush. Thereafter, as the yacht begins to drift away from the spot where the anchor is lying, more scope is paid out smoothly until enough is out for the anchor to work; in order to do this the pull of the cable must be at a flat angle along the seabed (Fig 24).

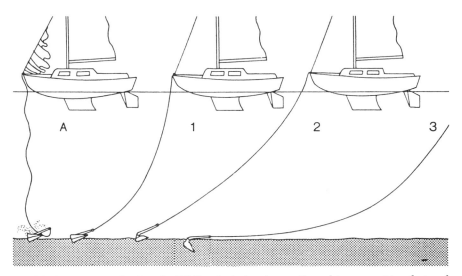

Fig 24 Stages in anchoring. In (A) the chain has been allowed to run out too fast and it has piled up on top of the anchor, possibly preventing it from working properly. In (1) the yacht is allowed to drift astern while chain is paid out smoothly and in (2) it is held by taking a turn or snubbing it to make the anchor take a bite. In (3) the yacht is out of sight but the anchor is beginning to bury itself safely.

It is dangerous to throw an anchor overboard. It must be passed out under the rail at the bows and over the fairlead and then simply released, either from the hands or by letting it dangle on its chain and releasing the chain or rope at the right moment. To throw an anchor is risky. A turn of cable could get round an ankle, with heaven knows what consequences, or it could become fouled up in its cable and refuse to work properly on the seabed.

Let us suppose that the water is ten metres deep. Down goes the anchor, we then pay out a total of thirty metres (more if we are using rope) as the boat drifts away, after which we 'snub' it. Snubbing an anchor means simply checking the cable by taking a turn round the cleat to tighten the cable and cause the anchor to bite into the seabed. The rest of the scope (the required length according to depth of water) is then let out and finally made fast properly. Sometimes a skipper likes to go astern on the engine to give it a good tug so that the point of the anchor digs home.

If there is a lot of wind and the yacht charges astern and brings up hard on her cable it is as well to watch for a while to ensure that she is not dragging. Look ashore and get any two marks (a tree on the shore and a distant house in the background, for instance) in line. If the yacht is dragging the marks will soon come out of line and the gap will steadily widen. This means that more

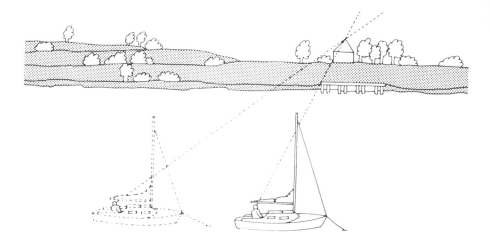

Fig 25 The observer in this yacht has taken marks ashore to see if she is dragging the anchor; the end of the jetty in line with the house gable. The dotted line boat shows how these marks would 'open' if she had dragged. Note: in gusts of strong wind there would be a bit of give and take causing the marks to shift in and out of line a small amount.

anchor scope is needed, or that she just is not going to hold at all and a fresh anchorage is needed (Fig 25).

Sometimes anchoring is a hectic business. In a fresh wind, a lumpy sea and maybe darkness and rain, when it is vital perhaps that the anchor bites first time and holds, the essential is to be sure that the cable will run smoothly up from its locker below without kinking, jamming or in any way preventing the anchor from doing its job. While the yacht is running towards the chosen anchorage, haul about ten metres of cable up on deck and then let it run back down again – this will clear any kinks.

In such circumstances the letting go will have to be done with great care to avoid the risk of injury. Everything will be heaving and crashing around and the boat will drift astern at great speed too, maybe off at an angle in a great clamour of shaking sails. The cable will have to be paid out very quickly and snubbing may have to be left until the full scope is out. What is important is that the final turns are taken before the weight of the boat comes on the cable. Once she lies back on the cable it will twang taut viciously and this can be dangerous to anyone who does not know what to expect. The best method is to pile three or four turns around the post and let her snub herself, then, when the cable slackens momentarily, the making fast part can be completed. In all probability, by this time the skipper will be assisting, but it is as well to know the drill.

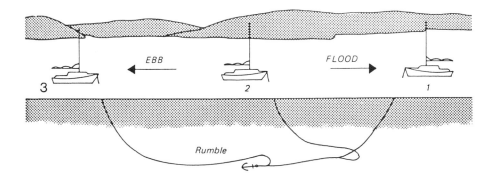

Fig 26 The alarming rumbles heard while anchored at night are usually caused by the chain dragging over itself at turn of the tide. In (1) the yacht is lying to the flood. In (2) the ebb is carrying her downstream over her anchor and the chain is rumbling. In (3) she is riding to the ebb and quiet again. If wind and tide are in opposition she may sheer around and rumble half the night. Rope anchor cables almost completely obviate this noise.

At anchor a yacht keeps up a series of swings and surges to and fro. At the turn of the tide the cable slackens and is dragged over the seabed before pulling from the opposite direction, and at every sudden change of wind the yacht alters the direction of the pull. All this means that anyone asleep below is subjected to a series of rumbles and clankings if the cable is chain, and it is easy to imagine that the anchor is dragging, as perhaps it is. I have always had a keen ear for a dragging anchor and turned my husband out at night on a number of occasions – and been proven right (Fig 26). Do not, on the other hand, take up a 'burglars in the kitchen' attitude. With experience you will learn what a dragging anchor really sounds like. The best way is to go and look, either at marks in line or at the cable. A dragging boat usually tightens her cable as she strains on it, then drags it with a rumble, whereupon it goes slack, then tightens and rumbles again and so on. This sequence also happens at times when the yacht has just swung and is taking up slack, so do not be fooled. Place a hand on the cable and feel the tension and the rumble. By lying below, knowing the state of wind and the tide and listening, a fair idea of what to expect can be gained.

All this perhaps is best left to the skipper until you have more experience. Remember, though, that to know is to be ready for the unexpected and that all boat knowledge is useful some time. More to the point is the drill for getting the anchor up. If the elements have combined to make this a physically difficult job it is really the skipper's responsibility and he will want it so, but now and then it becomes the mate's job – maybe in a slight emergency. The golden rule is to let the boat do the hardest work. Either she will be motored towards the anchor position while slack chain is hauled in, or it will be gathered in a series of easy hauls, waiting each time as the yacht strains back at it, taking a quick turn perhaps meanwhile. Once you have started the boat moving forward, continue to haul just hard enough to keep her going, paying the cable down its pipe into the locker as you go.

In due course the cable will come 'up and down', which is self-explanatory (Fig 27). If the anchor is firmly dug in it may be necessary to take a turn so that the weight of the yacht moving forward can snub its hold loose from the seabed. As soon as the hold breaks the boat is free to get under way, and in many cases there is not much time to waste in getting the boat going and under proper control, so the helmsman must be told at once. The rest of the job entails hauling up the anchor and getting it aboard carefully without banging hull or paintwork. It must then be lashed down in its chocks.

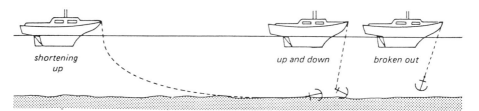

Fig 27 Stages in breaking out. Cable is shortened up until it is up-and-down, whereupon the anchor loses hold and breaks out.

A chain cable is much harder work to haul in when it comes to the final lift since you will be trying to haul up maybe ten metres of chain plus the anchor in a vertical lift. Many modern yachts, however, use a cable consisting of plaited nylon rope with a short length of chain, perhaps five metres, joining it to the anchor. This bit of chain provides weight to keep the pull horizontal and also takes care of much of the chafe against a rough seabed. Undoubtedly a rope cable is easier to haul in, although a yacht lying to rope tends to swing around rather more than one with an all-chain cable.

A cruiser in excess of 30 feet in length, if she has a small crew, may benefit by having an anchor windlass, certainly with an all-chain cable. Ideal too in bigger boats is some system of self-stowing anchor. This means that the anchor windlass is cranked away until the anchor is brought right up to deck level whereupon it slides neatly into its bow stowage.

Tripping lines

Some seabeds are littered with old junk, wreckage or rocks and an anchor can become jammed immovably under an old wire hawser. If a skipper has reason to suspect a 'foul' anchorage a tripping line and buoy may be used. A light but strong line is attached to the back of the anchor before letting go, the end of the line being marked by attaching a small buoy-marker. In the event of a foul the anchor can then be 'tripped' or pulled out backwards. However, this line can be a nuisance when raising the anchor because it may float back near the stern of the boat, and if the engine is running a fouled propeller might result. In weighing (raising) anchor, therefore, be ready with a boathook to lift the line aboard as soon as it is within reach.

In the section on letting go moorings, stress was laid on the importance of seeing that the boat is free to sail off in the desired direction – on one tack or the other, in fact. This is fairly easy to do when letting go a mooring, but at anchor it is not so simple. The anchor must not be broken out while the boat is heading in the wrong direction. Very likely the mainsail and the jib will be set – the latter getting in your way as it flogs around. The trick is to get the cable nearly up and down, then 'back' the jib against the wind so that it forces the yacht's bows in

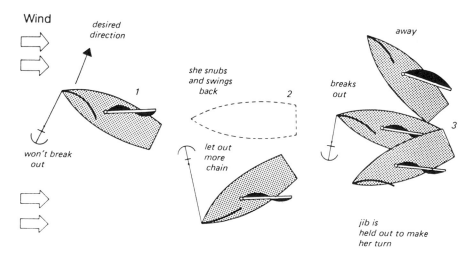

Fig 28 Breaking out under sail when the anchor refuses to let go. It is essential that the yacht pays off and begins moving (in this case towards the top of the page, or on port tack) in the desired direction. In (1) she refuses and the jerk of the cable turns her bow the wrong way. In (2) a little more cable is let go so that she does not break out and sail in the wrong direction. In (3) the jib is backed and slack cable gathered in quickly as she swings back yet again, and this time the anchor breaks out correctly.

the desired direction. The cable is then quickly hauled in and the anchor broken out in one movement (Fig 28). If by any chance it does not break its hold, the yacht will probably swing back on the wrong tack again. In which case, wait until she completes her swing. It may even be necessary to let go more chain, temporarily, just to hold her until she swings back again in the right direction. The second shot should be successful.

Since anchors dig deep into muddy seabeds and are often dirty when they come up, wear gloves to protect hands from this and from the rough ironwork, and try to keep the worst of the mud from coming on board. A nylon bristle pan brush attached to a stick about two feet long is useful. By leaving the anchor hanging just out of the water it is easy to reach over and scrub off the worst of the mud before lifting it aboard.

Handling ropes

In any small cruiser ropes need to be handled and the easiest way to spot a beginner is to see him, or her, pick up a coil of rope. The crux of the matter is that word 'coil'. The only way a rope can be picked up and remain ready for use is in a coil, otherwise it becomes a tangle. The experienced yachtsman cannot tolerate a rope that is not coiled and his first instinctive reaction is to coil it, or if it has been badly coiled, to re-coil it.

There are all sorts of lines and ropes in a yacht. Halliards, when the sails are set, offer a mass of slack rope on deck; mainsheets become a muddle in the cockpit and so does the lee jib sheet, which can also create a lot of slack end to lie around. Then there are warps for mooring or anchoring, heaving lines (more about them later) and many more shorter bits and pieces of rope. If ropes are not tidy and an emergency crops up, chaos soon reigns. An untidy, loose end can fall overboard and get wrapped around the propeller, for instance, or a sheet become knotted which prevents the sail from being let out – perhaps during a squall when it has become vital to spill wind. A rope lying around on deck will also roll beneath the foot if trodden on and could cause someone to slip and possibly fall overboard.

Certain types of rope are easier to coil than others, but the standing rule with all ordinary rope is to coil it clockwise. Imagine taking the end of a rope and laying it on the floor in a circle, feeding the rope round in the same direction as the hands of a clock – this is the way to coil a large, heavy warp. Now imagine picking up the coil and holding it in your hand, continuing to make clockwise circles with the other, turn after turn until the rope is coiled (Fig 29).

Depending on the thickness of the rope, the size or diameter of the coil is varied. A small coil, about the size of a dinner plate, is about right for a rope as thick as a pencil, with progressively larger coils for thicker rope. The aim is to make the smallest coil to which the rope will *naturally* lend itself. The halliards and sheets in a small cruiser will be about half an inch thick and the best coil will be about twelve inches in diameter, though this is a very wide generality.

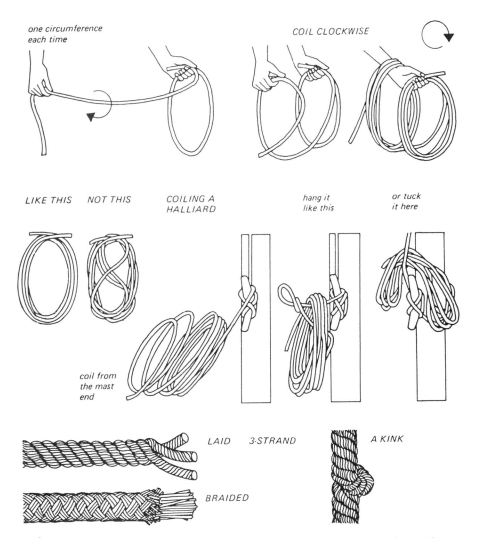

Fig 29 Coiling. It is essential to develop a mechanical hand movement when coiling lines. Each turn should lie naturally over the previous one if the rope is free of twists and kinks. The lower diagrams show examples of laid 3-strand rope and braided rope. Any kink in a rope must be removed at once; it could easily jam and stop a sail being lowered or a sheet eased out.

Incidentally, the end of a halliard or sheet which is in use should not be coiled from its idle end; it must be coiled from where it is attached to winch or cleat.

Rope may be three strand or plaited. Nowadays it will almost certainly be of Nylon, or Terylene, or some other synthetic, and although it is easier to handle and kinder on the hands than old fashioned hemp, manila or sisal, it can still become kinked. A kink, as everyone knows, is a sharp twist which results from a tangle or from a coil which has got itself round the wrong way. It is worth knowing that if a kink is allowed to stay in a rope, and that rope comes under a

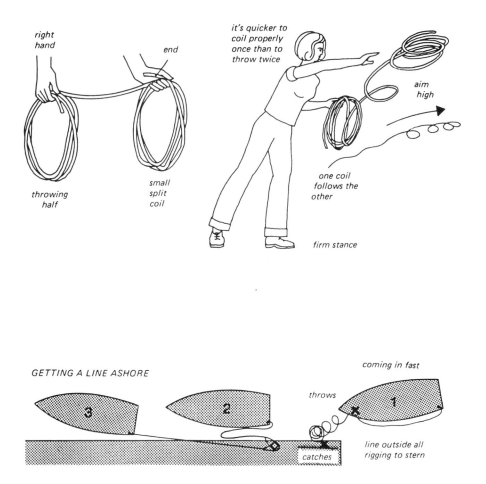

Fig 30 Careful coiling is the secret when throwing a heaving line. Divide the coil as shown and remember to aim high. There's a knack to throwing a line and it needs practice. When approaching a dock try to get the stern line fast first if there is going to be difficulty in slowing the yacht. If it is made fast aft and led outside all rigging to the bow and thrown ashore from there, it will give the person ashore more time for making fast before the strain comes on it.

sudden heavy strain, the actual strength at that point can be reduced by half. This means that when rope is coiled all the kinks must be removed from it. (Coiling three-strand 'right-handed' rope the wrong way i.e., anti-clockwise, actually puts kinks into it.) The knack is to take the coil in the left hand and build up the turns with the right hand, if right-handed, occasionally giving the slack rope a spin to remove the kinks as they appear.

One of the surest tests of a well coiled rope is when the coil has to be thrown or 'heaved'. If the yacht is manoeuvring to go alongside a quay, perhaps, the moment will come when she is near enough for the line to be thrown to the shore. The line which is to be thrown will usually be a light mooring rope which is supple and easy to coil. I have my own favourite line which I guard jealously. A heaving line should be coiled fairly small – large dinner plate size is about right. Coil it carefully allowing no kinks to creep in. When ready to heave the thrower takes the coil in one hand and divides it so that half the coil is now in the other. The coil must be divided exactly right – just as if a coil bed-spring had been stretched into two parts. The thrower makes sure there is clear deck behind and that the feet are well braced, then swings the throwing arm back and heaves half the coil up and away. If all goes well the airborne coil will extend smoothly and the rest of the coil, held loosely in the other hand, will follow turn upon turn. Do not let go of the end, of course, and to be on the safe side it is best to stand on it or tie it round something on deck (Fig 30). If the mate can master the art of throwing a heaving line, the whole business of going alongside becomes much simpler and far less strain on the skipper.

While on the subject of going alongside, we will finish dealing with the use of ropes for this purpose. If the line has been heaved and caught by someone ashore the skipper will probably ask them to make it fast or take a turn round a post, bollard or ring. The yacht will have been going ahead and the rope will be used to stop her progress. In a small cruiser the heaving line will also serve as a warp for the purpose of stopping, but in a bigger boat it would be used to send a much thicker rope to the person ashore, who hauls in the thin line to get to the thick one. This assumes that there is someone ashore ready to catch your line and make it fast. This is not always the case. How to jump ashore when coming alongside is dealt with in Chapter 8.

Once the line is made fast ashore, you will be told to take it to the bow or the stern quickly. What is vital is that the end is passed *under* the rail and in through one of the fairleads and thence to a large enough cleat or post on deck. This must be done and a turn taken before the strain comes on the rope. If the boat is moving too fast it is necessary to 'surge' the turn, which means that the turns round the post or cleat are allowed to slip around a little. This eases the load on the rope, which might otherwise be enough to snap it. Sometimes, in a real

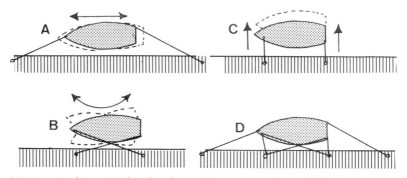

Fig 31 Mooring lines. (A): head and stern lines restrict fore and aft movement. (B): springs limit slewing effect. (C): breast lines hold the yacht at a fixed distance from the jetty. (D): fully moored.

panic, there may not be time to pass the line under the rail properly, in which case the urgent thing is to stop the headway by taking that turn. Fingers must be kept well clear, or they could get damaged. Once the boat has been checked the procedure for mooring up follows, passing various ropes and lines from ship to shore. This is one of those techniques best learned by helping a few times (Fig 31).

Knots, hitches and bends

You cannot get away with even the most basic crewing for long without learning at least one or two knots, hitches or bends. We generalize wrongly by calling them all 'knots', just as we speak of 'tying' them instead of 'making' them, but this is perhaps the counsel of perfection.

Let us content ourselves with learning just six knots: the reef knot, bowline, figure-of-eight, round turn and two half hitches, sheet bend and clove hitch. Of these the reef knot, figure-of-eight and round turn and two half hitches will take precedence, but for good and useful crewing all should be learned (Fig 32).

Just as important as knowing how to make the knots is knowing when to use them. The reef knot is used for joining the ends of two lines of equal thickness, and like all correctly tied knots it has the virtue of being easy to untie. Incidentally, a point about knots in synthetic rope; do not use the very ends of the lines. This type of rope is sometimes limp and slippery and knots are liable to come undone easily and quite accidentally. If the knots are vitally important – say in the case of a rope being made fast (or bent on as we say) to an anchor, make extra sure by also tying the end to the main rope with a piece of string. This is known as 'seizing the end'.

The bowline is a loop or 'bight' which will not slip and it is used in the end of a

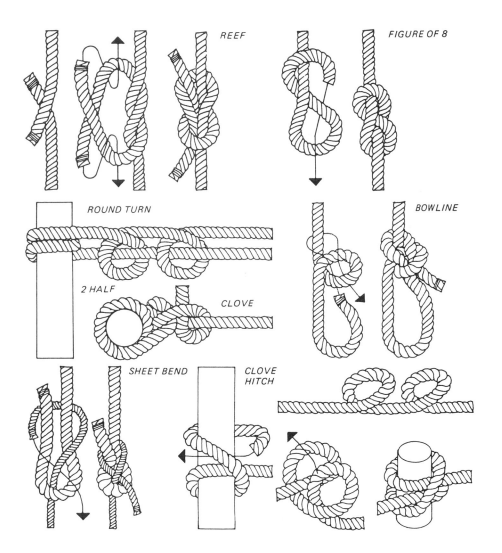

Fig 32 A reef knot correctly tied will have both short ends on the same side. The figure-of-eight is a 'stopper' knot and easy to untie. A round turn and two half hitches has a great many uses; note that the half hitches actually form a clove hitch (see below). The bowline is a non-slip loop or bight which remains easy to untie. Sheet bends are used to join a thick line to a thinner one; leave plenty of loose end or it may shake itself loose. A clove hitch can either be tied round a post or bar or made by forming two turns as shown and dropping them over a post. Synthetic ropes tend to be slippery or springy in some cases and prone to untying themselves; leave plenty of slack end and always pull knots really tight. Never make knots in chain or wire.

rope or warp which goes over a bollard or post for mooring the boat to a quay, etc. The figure-of-eight is a 'stopper' knot and used at the end of both jib sheets and the mainsheet so that they cannot be jerked out of their fairleads or run through their blocks. It is easy to untie in a hurry and makes a nice big knob. When a rope, such as a dinghy painter or bow rope, has to be made fast to the yacht or to a jetty, the round turn and two half hitches is the safest and easiest knot to use. Usually it becomes a half turn and two half hitches, but the important thing is that the hitches are both made in the same direction.

The sheet bend is for joining the end of two ropes of different thickness as a rule. Be sure to use the thicker end as shown, or the knot will fail. If the ropes are very different in thickness, it is best to be on the safe side and make a double sheet bend by passing the short end of the thinner line under the thicker part twice. The clove hitch is often used instead of the round turn and two half hitches when securing the dinghy, but again do not make it in the very end of the rope; it could work its way round and slip.

Thumb knots, the over and under knot, should never be used as they are difficult to untie and anyway they serve no purpose. On the other hand, they often appear accidentally in coils of rope and should be undone at once before they tighten up. Another traditionally forbidden knot is the half-hitch by itself used on a cleat. Once the rope comes under strain the hitch cannot be undone. Even with two or three turns of rope made fast figure-of-eight fashion around the cleat beforehand, the half hitch should not be used with natural fibre ropes. When these get wet they swell and the hitch jams. Incidentally synthetic ropes do not swell, which brings us to the exception to the rule. In modern yachts, many of which have small cleats, synthetic rope tends to come undone and now and again a half hitch to hold the turns in place is an advantage.

Practise the knots in thick rope and thin and learn how to tie them blindfold – sooner or later they will have to be made in the dark. Learn to heave a line and coil a rope quickly and know which knots to use and you will be regarded with respect by experienced sailors.

The echosounder

Years ago a heavy weight on a marked line – the 'leadline' – was used for measuring depth of water and it was a wet and messy business. It was also slow, and between one sounding and the next, after hauling, and recoiling, and throwing again (heaving the lead as it was called) the yacht might have sailed hard aground. Echosounders have changed all that. An electronic pulse is sent downwards from a transducer in the bottom of the boat, the pulse hits the bottom and echoes back while the instrument registers the time taken in the form of a depth reading.

Some echosounders are more sophisticated in having a pre-set alarm facility. This means that if you want to be warned when the boat is approaching shallow water it can be adjusted to, say, ten metres, and thereafter you have no need to watch it because a loud buzzer will sound if that depth is reached. A maximum depth setting can also be used to tell you when the depth increases to a pre-set sounding. One thing to watch, however, is the chance of a false echo – a shoal of fish, a layer of suspended silt or even a temperature layer underwater can cause this, but provided you know roughly what the depth is likely to be from the chart, a false echo is usually spotted for what it is.

Reading the echosounder is very simple, but for the person assigned to it there is still a right and wrong way to do the job. The skipper will want to know the depths (always assuming that he cannot see the instrument) at regular intervals and it is an annoyance to have to keep asking for a reading. Whether the reading alters or not, keep announcing the depths in steady succession, about every five to ten seconds, until told to stop or to note only alterations. Supposing there had been a steady ten metres for some time, the skipper would want to be told of any shoaling or deepening, and the steeper the rise or fall the more rapidly the soundings should be read out. Speak clearly, with any navigational uncertainty skippers tend to become a bit edgy despite often presenting a facade of unruffled calm.

Secure for the night

When a cruiser comes to anchor for the night there are many things to be done after she has been securely anchored. Usually this is the point at which the cook goes below and begins to think about food. But if there is a plan to eat ashore it is a case of all hands on deck to snug the ship down.

The sails must be properly stowed, with headsails bagged and sent to their stowage space. There are various ideas for stowing a mainsail. Some people do not bother much about neatness and simply put a few lashings or tyers on, then secure the sail coat over all. A good sail stow is worth doing though. Not only does it look neat and seamanlike, but the sail is secure should it come on to blow during the night (Fig 33).

The battens may or may not be taken out. Personally I believe in leaving them in because one never knows when it may be necessary to get under way in the dark – and quickly at that. First the sail, which is still hanked to both the boom and the mast, is pulled over to one side, then the leech (the back edge) is

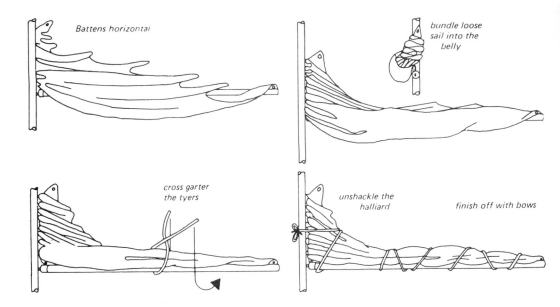

Fig 33 Stowing a mainsail. If the battens are to be left ready for instant use the folds of sail must first be gathered so that the battens are horizontal to the boom. The foot of the sail is formed into a bag and the rest of the material is bundled into it. Finally it is rolled tight and secured by tyers as shown. It may be necessary to take the top batten out for a really neat stow, otherwise it could get broken.

pulled forward on top of the boom and the bottom part of the loose sail is drawn out sideways and held to make a sort of bag into which all the loose sail is tumbled. This can then be rolled up and the tyers made fast.

The introduction of mast rolling/reefing mainsails, of course, obviates any need to stow a sail on the boom since the whole thing (like a roller jib) rolls up inside the hollow mast. Likewise with a roller reefing boom, many people simply rotate the boom until the whole sail is wound up on it. I am not too keen on this because it means that if the sail needed to be hoisted quickly time would be lost having to feed the sail slides back into the groove on the mast.

Jib sheets must be secured each side and coiled, so must the mainsheet. There may be a prop, or crutch, into which the boom is lowered, if not then the topping lift is adjusted so that the boom is 'topped up' high enough to clear heads and the boom sheeted down to hold it secure. Halliards are pulled tight and secured by the 'crane lines' which pull them away from the mast.

The bilges may need pumping after a hard sail; there may be a bow fender to sling (a special type which hangs under the bow like a necklace and keeps the chain away from the hull) and a couple of ordinary fenders may be hung alongside the cockpit for the dinghy to lie alongside. If it is an inflatable dinghy it can be allowed to bump without risk of damage to the yacht. Take any loose gear such as oars out of it because inflatables can be blown over by a gust of wind if there is no weight in them. Remember to take the outboard motor off as well because this *can* damage topsides. Its weight also cocks the dinghy bows up a little and makes her even more vulnerable to sudden gusts of wind in the night.

In the case of a rigid wooden or glassfibre dinghy things are a bit different. The dinghy may need bailing out if it has been towed. If it is to be left afloat for the night it may be either moored against fenders and secured bow and stern, or secured astern on its painter. In the latter case it may be a good idea to take the deck bucket on its line and make it fast to the stern of the dinghy, allowing the bucket to sink. This cuts down the risk of the dinghy becoming a nuisance in the night if at any time the wind and tide should be in opposition. Being subject to the wind rather than the tide, the dinghy could come ranging up and hit the anchored yacht again and again. The bucket, dragged by the current, reduces the likelihood of this.

If the yacht is at anchor in, say, a river, the riding light must be rigged. This is a light which can be seen from all around and which is required by law to show that the boat is at anchor. If somebody ran into you in the dark and you were not showing a riding light you might lose an insurance claim. The light may be a permanent feature or it may be plugged in and tied to the forestay as high as you can reach.

All in all quite a lot of work, to say nothing of the extra small repairs which may be required – engine maintenance and so on – before snugging down. But for all that there are few things as satisfying as snugging down for the night in some quiet anchorage.

Back in home port

When it comes to leaving the boat on her moorings or in her berth after a cruise (or even an afternoon sail), the deck tasks mentioned above have to be tackled as well as securing the boat below decks. The gas must be turned off at its bottle and the pipes burned out, seacocks turned off and engine ignition and all electrics switched off. Bilges must be pumped out, hatches secured and ventilators left so that some air current can circulate below. It is a good idea to have a permanent checklist fixed in the companionway and facing you as you leave the boat. This way the vital jobs do not get overlooked.

7 A STAGE FURTHER

The more sailing skills you learn the smoother the management of the yacht will be and the happier all concerned. More to the point, the safer everyone becomes, because in a small cruiser the concentration of all skills in one person is rather a hazardous arrangement. In this chapter we become more deeply involved in the handling and general management of the boat at sea.

Reefing

If the mate was left alone on watch and a sudden thunder squall struck without warning, he or she might be faced with a sudden need to reduce sail area. The obvious first means of reducing sail is to let fly the sheets or, if the boat was close-hauled, to luff still closer spilling wind yet keeping the boat under control. If she was on a dead run and perhaps in a narrow channel neither of these remedies would be possible. Letting fly sheets in a squall is in any case a very temporary measure because the violence of flapping sails will very soon cause damage.

Another measure, if the yacht has a roller headsail, is to roll it up and sail under mainsail alone while heading up close-hauled. In fact, a yacht hard on the wind under main only, perhaps with the engine at half speed, is a very effective combination, although again of little help if running.

The real answer is to reef the sails well in advance of trouble. The boat is headed up onto a close reach and sheets eased to slow her. In some yachts all reefing can be done without leaving the cockpit, but failing this the procedure is as follows. With roller boom reefing the plan is to ease away the mainsail halliard so that the sail slides down its track, whilst at the same time winding the reefing handle to rotate the boom, and wrapping the sail round it. Usually the sheet is eased right off allowing the sail to shake while this is being done, but some rigs work best with a little wind in the sail. Roller reefing is not always very efficient because it causes wrinkles to form in the sail and sometimes allows

Taking a slab-reef down. The reef pennant which pulls down the 'clew' of the sail emerges from the boom near the mast and this mate is hauling it down by means of the small winch. Once properly tight she will lock it fast by means of a jamming device, see X.

A slab-reef hauled down and with the loose bunt of sail tidied up by means of rubber cord. Note the clean, flat set of the sail. The rope disappearing upwards in the right of the picture is the upper reef pennant.

the end of the boom to droop. Having rolled down the required amount of sail
the halliard must be set up again. If there is a kicking strop fitted this may have
to be removed for the boom to roll. Some boats also have a 'claw ring' fitting to
which the sheet attaches and this too can complicate things.

A better reefing system is the slab-reef. Here the sail is lowered until a large
eyelet, or thimble, can be dropped over a hook on the boom close to the mast.
The halliard is then hardened up. Now the outer end of the sail must be pulled
down to the boom and this is done by hauling on the reef pennant. There are
generally two of these, one for the first reef and a second higher up the sail for a
deeper reef. Usually the boom will have a special clamping device for holding
these pennants. The pennants will be 'rove' (threaded) inside the boom
emerging via a clamp, so that having hauled the pennant as tight as it will go
the clamp lever has only to be pushed over to lock it. Some booms also have a
small winch to assist in this hauling process. Having hauled down the forward
edge of the sail, hooked it on and then hauled down the outer edge of the sail the
reef is virtually complete. There will be some arrangement of lines or rubber
cord for tidying up the loose sail, but if time presses this can be left until later.

A roller headsail can be half-rolled to reduce area although it is rarely as
effective as changing to a smaller headsail. Some boats have a staysail which
can be set with the jib rolled up out of the way, but faced with a need to sail hard
to windward to reach shelter in a rising wind a well reefed mainsail plus the
engine (as mentioned earlier) is probably the best compromise.

Heaving-to

Knowing how to slow down and to stop a boat is very important. When people
are working on deck, for instance, slowing the boat by carefully easing off the
sheets until the sails are just fluttering will reduce the jerky motion and stop
spray from coming aboard. Likewise if the boat is lying beam-on to the waves
and rolling violently, hardening in the mainsheet a little and pointing the boat a
little towards the waves will give her an easier motion.

In an emergency (see Chapter 13) stopping the boat altogether by heaving-to
also means that the boat can be left with no one at the helm. Heaving-to in this
way can also be useful if you need time to take careful navigational checks and,
of course, being able to stop the boat has vital implications in the case of man
overboard.

In a moderate or light breeze most boats will lie quietly if laid beam-on to the
wind with sails completely free and shaking. Slow the yacht right down first by
easing sheets and as soon as most of her forward way has been lost you should

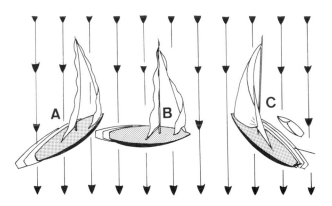

Fig 34 In (A) the yacht is slowed by luffing into the wind with sheets eased so that the sails shake. On a beam reach (B) with sheets eased she will probably lie almost stopped and needing nobody at the helm. In (C) she has hove-to; the mainsail is close-hauled, the jib is backed and the tiller is down tending to steer her into the wind. The opposing forces of mainsail and backed jib produce a stalemate situation and the yacht drifts quietly with helm unattended.

be able to leave the tiller while she lies rolling gently and drifting forwards and sideways (Fig 34).

To heave-to, however, the sails are used. With the boat roughly close-hauled, pull the jib across so that it is *backed*, that is to say it is on the wrong side. Alternatively tacking the boat without altering the jib sheets across leaves the jib aback. The effect is for the mainsail to be pushing the bows round into the wind while the backed jib is trying to push them away from the wind; with one sail counterbalancing the other the result is a stalemate in which the boat is heeling under full sail but more or less stationary. In order to hold her there the tiller will have to be held or lashed *down*, or in other words lashed to a cleat or something on the *lee side* of the cockpit.

In practice, and dependent upon the strength of the wind and size of jib carried, experimentation with the sheets may be needed to get the balance right, but usually if the clew of the jib is level with the mast and the mainsheet is not hard in, the boat will take up an angle midway betwen close-hauled and reaching and just forge ahead slowly, drifting sideways a little at the same time. Heaving-to is usually carried out when it is necessary to wait for a while, perhaps off a river entrance when awaiting deeper water on a bar or entry signals off a harbour mouth. However, if crew go below and leave the deck unwatched for brief periods the direction of drift, tide-set and so on must be noted, particularly if a lee-shore is nearby or if there is traffic about. Usually a yacht is hove-to on starboard tack to give her right of way over other sailing craft according to the sailing rules. It is far safer to leave one crew on watch whatever the circumstances.

Some boats will even heave-to under mainsail only or jib only if the tiller is lashed, but this can only be found by experiment and it may work in a light wind but not in a strong one.

The night watch

While the possibility of an emergency in which the mate has to take over the whole show must always be considered, it is happily a remote exigency; more immediate is the mate's value if she can manage the ship while the skipper can get some rest. Anyone who has sailed offshore knows how difficult it is to sleep unless one has complete confidence in those on deck and their ability to cope with big ship traffic, or handle the yacht in variations of wind strength and direction. Only when a skipper knows that the mate on deck is fully capable of reacting confidently to the changing situation and is experienced enough to recognize a potential emergency, and will call him, can he rest with an easy mind.

The first night at sea is the greatest adventure. It may also be cold and frightening. The skipper may decide to stay up all night and leave the crew to sail the boat in daylight while he sleeps a little, or he may sleep for an hour or two before midnight if all seems to be well. In normal weather and with a small crew of perhaps a man and wife, a child and maybe one other adult, the skipper may elect to take the middle of the night watch (from 11 P.M., to 3 A.M.) letting the others share the remainder of the dark hours. If the other adult is experienced they might well share the whole night between them, or give the wife the first watch from dusk to 11 P.M. but if the extra adult is inexperienced the wife will be the watch officer and the skipper will rest 'on call'.

Without doubt the most important of all night duties is to watch for ships. The course must be steered and a keen eye kept for changes of wind, but the vital matter is to see that the yacht is sailed safely past big shipping.

Around the coasts of every well-populated country ships pass in steady succession. They converge at major headlands and in the vicinity of ports and navigable rivers, and they follow distinct 'lanes' at sea. At the Straits of Dover, for instance, something like seven hundred large ships pass every twenty-four hours. Traffic separation zones exist in very busy waters in which vessels on opposing courses are divided. Rules must be known and obeyed.

It is a widely held belief that power driven vessels must always give way to sailing vessels; while this is so (Rule 18 International Regulations for Preventing Collisions at Sea 1972) there are other circumstances in which it simply does not apply. Apart from these exceptions it is not by any means certain that a big powered vessel will get out of the way of a tiny sailing craft. They give way if they can and if they can *see you*. Some try to shave past close without altering course; others may *appear* to give way, but in fact are really swerving to and fro due to difficulty in steering which is caused by their being in ballast, or unloaded, and high in the water. Some alter course because they have spotted another large ship, way beyond the small yacht which they may well not have

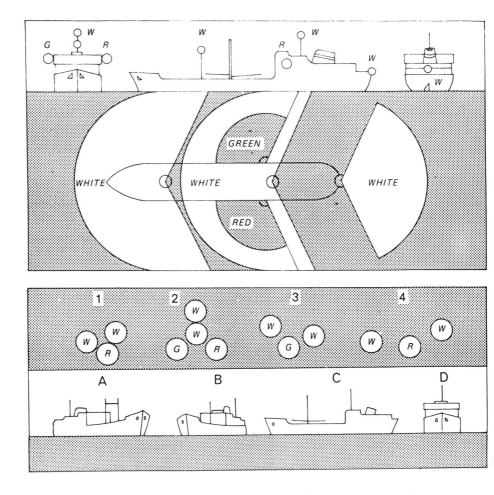

Fig 35 Lights and shipping. Memorize the positions of lights on this typical steamer and then try to visualize the angle at which the ship is lying from the 'lights' shown in the black strip. See if you can match them up with the ships at the bottom. (Answers at the end of the Chapter.)

seen. The important thing is to keep a very close watch on any ship until her lights show that she is safely past, in case she alters course suddenly just when you assumed her to be well clear.

The lights carried by ships must be understood and they are really very simple to grasp. Every powered vessel over 50 metres must carry two white masthead lights in addition to port and starboard lights; the latter must be visible from ahead to 22.5° abaft the beam. This means that the red port light, for instance, cannot be seen from starboard, but on the port side it can be seen until she passes from broadside-on to a little ahead of this point. From then on her white stern light becomes visible. The two white mast-head lights, one slightly forward and lower than the other, can be seen from all angles until the ship is past the broad-side-on position and beginning to move away. When she is past, only her stern light can be seen.

Thus, by mentally sorting out the lights seen and their relative positions to each other, it is possible to judge whether a ship is passing on a parallel course, moving away, coming head-on or approaching at an angle on a converging course – which may or may not be a collision course! The diagrams in Fig 35 include a simple test; have a good look at them and see if you can judge the courses of the ships concerned.

The distance and speed of ships is difficult to assess at first. One moment it is a distant twinkle of lights, the next they are high up and glowing brightly. The white lights are seen first, then the coloured ones, and finally lights from portholes and elsewhere can be seen reflected in the water. By now the ship will be so close that the yacht should not be on anything approaching a collision course. If in doubt it is a safe plan to call the skipper when the coloured lights become visible. If both coloured lights can be seen at the same time, but very small and distant, it will mean that, providing you are moving nicely, you have passed ahead, but *watch that ship closely*. If you continue to see both coloured lights she is coming straight at you. Always note how wide apart the white masthead lights appear because when they draw close together the ship is heading your way.

There is a simple trick for estimating a collision course (Fig 36). Steer the yacht as straight as possible and sit quite still. Find some object on the yacht, such as a winch or stay, which is in line with the lights of the converging steamer. Do this when she is still a very long way off. Keeping your head quite still, if it is a collision course, then the ship, the object and your eye will remain in line as the two vessels draw closer; if they come out of line and you are certain your course has been straight it is fairly safe to assume that all is well. But *watch her*. This trick does not work so well if you are both approaching at a narrow angle or in rough conditions.

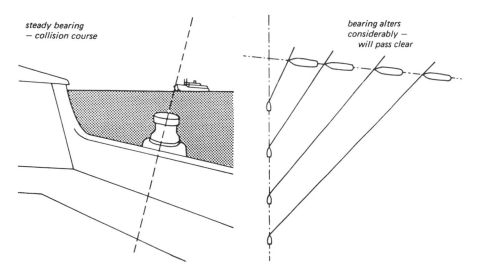

Fig 36 Collision course. By keeping the steamer in line with some part of the yacht while steering a dead straight course and sitting still, you can see whether the steamer will pass clear or whether the two craft are on a collision course.

Never be slow to call the skipper from below in uncertain situations – even if he is very tired and only just gone to sleep.

Rules of the road at sea

Anyone in charge of a boat at sea should know the Collision Regulations – the highway code of the sea. Just as important, anyone who is likely to be left at the helm should have an understanding of the basic rules at least. Another vessel, hitherto passing safely, may suddenly alter course, and a split-second decision to avoid a collision may be vital. Briefly, here are the important points to watch.

Big ships must always be regarded seriously. The old basic rule 'power gives way to sail' is hard to enforce and no longer always applies. Never pass close ahead of a big ship although it may be your right technically. You can never be 100 per cent certain that you have been seen. In fact never rely upon being seen in the open sea at night. Keep clear of big shipping channels and restricted waters; sudden and violent course changes may be necessary as the ship manoeuvres to follow a narrow channel, so give plenty of sea room.

The 'shipping lanes' or separation lanes referred to are marked on the charts very plainly and usually occur wherever there are large concentrations of ships. If possible we try to avoid them rather than cross them, but this is not always

Bearing away to pass the stern of a ship. This had been a collision situation in the making until the yacht skipper took the wise option. Such changes of course, though, should be made boldly and decisively so that intention is plain.

possible. A separation zone consists of two separate wide (several miles) lanes with a no-go strip in between, rather like motorway traffic moving in one way streams – east-going or west-going maybe. A small vessel, whether sailing or power, *must not* hamper the movements of large ships in such lanes, and if crossing them must cross as near as possible at right angles to the oncoming ships; heavy fines can be imposed upon wrong doers. As such, lanes are usually under radar surveillance; 'Big Brother' is watching.

When we have to cross such lanes we usually motor unless sailing fast and at the correct angle. Quite often ships in a lane will form a procession and it can be difficult to dodge a way through them. It sometimes pays to wait just outside the edge of the lane, perhaps for half an hour because ships tend to bunch together as cars do on a motorway.

Under sail the starboard tack boat has precedence whether running (boom out to port), reaching or close-hauled. When two sailing boats have the wind on the same side the vessel which is to windward must keep clear. The overtaking vessel, on any point of sailing, must keep clear of those it overtakes. Racing yachts (those flying the square burgee) sail to a more complicated set of rules and to avoid spoiling their sport other vessels usually give them right of way. However it is worth noting that this is a courtesy gesture only.

In channels keep to the starboard side when approaching another vessel head-on, but do not cut across its bows in order to get to the starboard side. If you are passing safely, hold your course. Consider whether there is a bend in the channel and whether the other ship (if large) is likely to make an alteration of course which will conflict with yours.

If the engine is on (whether the sails are set or not) a boat is classed as a powered vessel and must give way to *all* craft under sail. A vessel under power gives way to other power vessels approaching and converging from the starboard side unless that vessel is the overtaking one. Once again it is up to the overtaking vessel to keep clear of those it overtakes. When approaching head-on at sea, turn to starboard a little to pass port to port.

Large ships blow their sirens to signal their intentions to turn. One blast means 'I am altering course to starboard', two blasts 'I am altering course to port', and three blasts 'my engines are going astern'. If a ship blows five short blasts, beware; she may be saying 'You are in danger of colliding with me'. In some rivers, however, four blasts followed by either one or two blasts means that the ship is about to turn completely round to port or starboard.

In any situation involving big ships and yachts we have to remember that a yacht is not always visible even in daylight. A hazy, sunny day can render a white yacht with white sails almost invisible at a range of a mile or so, and on a rough day with lots of white wavecrests and poor visibility even radar may fail to detect a yacht amongst the reflected wave clutter. Remember also that from the bridge of a ship the view ahead is often limited by the ship's bows so that a yacht dead ahead can be lost to view if she gets too close. Bear this in mind when in the vicinity of shipping.

The tides

The behaviour of the tides is a truly vast subject about which whole books have been written. I will therefore leave out much of the technical and scientific stuff and deal with the sort of tidal knowledge which I have assimilated through practical sailing experience.

Obedient to the pull of sun and moon the surface of the world's seas and oceans is lifted and, as the earth spins, a very shallow tidal wave runs round the globe. In shallow waters and in confined waters, such as the English Channel, the tidal wave builds up into a bigger concentration of water. An extreme case is the Bristol Channel where the funnel effect of the narrowing river causes a tidal 'bore', which actually becomes a wall of water several feet high as the tide builds up. All this means is that some places have a low rise and fall of tide while others have a much larger one.

Tides do not always reach their highest level at each high water time. Week and week about there are neap tides – which are lower ones – and spring tides which rise higher. This is due to the amount of pull exerted by the sun and moon when working either together or against each other. Several times each year come the really big tides and the equinoctial periods. There are two high waters in each twenty four hours, but because the cycles of low water to high water and back to low water occupy a little more than twelve hours, the times of high water are slightly later each day. For example, it might be high water at 8 A.M. today in a certain place, but tomorrow it might be high water at, say, 8.50 A.M., and so on.

Because the tidal stream floods along the coasts and up the rivers and then ebbs back again, the times of high water vary from port to port all over the world. In England, to save having hundreds of tide tables, all tides are based on 'High Water Dover' in home waters and we add or subtract a little to find the high water times for other places. Other countries have their own 'standard' ports.

There is one other aspect of tidal rise and fall which is important. The water level does not creep up and down at the same speed. After low water it begins to rise slowly at first then quicker and quicker until the middle of the rise, after which the rate of rise slows down again. The same thing happens in reverse on the ebb.

To 'catch a tide', therefore, is to be in the right place when the current is beginning to go the way you want to go, and to have a 'foul' tide is to have it against you. It can also catch you sideways and set you off course unless a course is planned which allows for this.

There is one hoary old misconception which even trips up people who should know better; novelists fall for it in droves. If someone said that a yacht was becalmed and not moving and the boathook which fell overboard was *taken out of reach by the tide*, they would be talking nonsense. Unless the yacht was anchored, both it and the boathook would be moving together on the tide. It is like sitting in a chair in the middle of a carpet which is slowly being towed along. A dropped book would lie by your chair where it fell, despite the fact that both you and the book were being towed.

Being aware of the importance of tides makes us more willing to shape our on-shore excursions to suit the situation and to understand why the engine may have to be started at sea sometimes and why it is often impossible to arrive at a destination at the expected time.

Understanding the tides means we put our knowledge to good effect. If shopping has to be done by dinghy we must know where to leave it, what the tide is doing when we go ashore and what it is likely to be doing when ready to return. This might mean pulling the dinghy well up the slipway before securing the painter, otherwise a flooding tide could put it out of reach later on. We might time the row ashore so that the current is with us each way. Likewise we can row carefully along the shallow edges of the shore or river banks where the current is slackest to avoid a hard pull, and on returning later row right down the middle in deep water to get the full benefit of the favourable current. This is practical tidal lore (Fig 37).

When at sea, at the tiller, mentally review the tidal situation when passing navigational buoys (Fig 38). When sailing across the tide a buoy must be passed *down tide* unless it can be passed *well up tide*, otherwise the yacht may be swept on to it and possibly suffer serious damage. Anything anchored or moored or sticking up from the seabed must be watched with caution in a tideway – other vessels which are *not* moored will be moving on the same tidal stream (the carpet).

The relation of tidal rise and fall to the figures of depth shown on the chart is a complicated business and well worth learning in due course. At this point

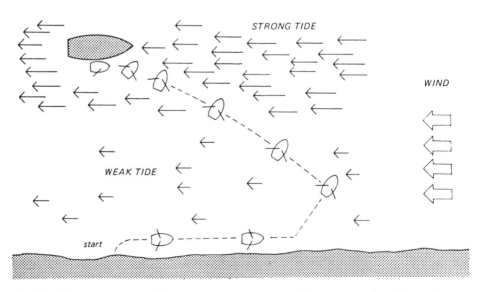

Fig 37 This rower, faced with a strong cross wind and tide, is going about things the sensible way. She has rowed well upstream close to the shore where the current is generally weaker, and in due course cuts across rowing crab-wise, finally rowing head to tide and wind, allowing them to drop her down to the moored craft. Note that she goes alongside well towards the bow.

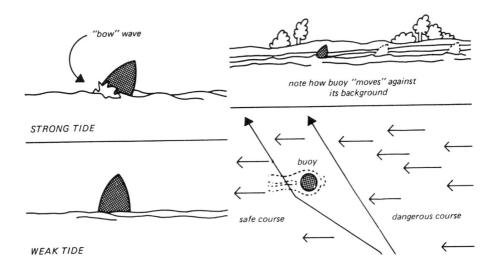

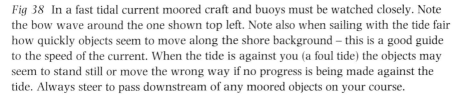

Fig 38 In a fast tidal current moored craft and buoys must be watched closely. Note the bow wave around the one shown top left. Note also when sailing with the tide fair how quickly objects seem to move along the shore background – this is a good guide to the speed of the current. When the tide is against you (a foul tide) the objects may seem to stand still or move the wrong way if no progress is being made against the tide. Always steer to pass downstream of any moored objects on your course.

though, it will suffice to generalize. When passing a buoy which can be identified on the chart, a reading on the echosounder makes it possible to compare the depth found with the depth shown for that position on the chart. This is usually deeper than indicated on the chart, since those depths charted amount to the level at very low tides.

By looking up the time of high water for the area it will be possible to see whether it is high water, or at some stage in between. Having ascertained that there is (probably) more water under us than the chart shows at that spot, we now can tell whether we expect still more depth (tide is flooding) or whether the level is going to fall until it becomes more like the figures given on the chart (tide is ebbing). All this touches on whether it is safe to carry on into shallower water or whether the yacht should head for deeper water.

When anchoring a yacht at high tide, it is important to know whether she will stay afloat at low tide. For example the tide tables may show a particular tide has a height of 4 metres; there is only 5 metres of water and our yacht needs 1 metre to float in. It might seem that we are exactly right and that her keel will just touch at low tide. This is the tricky part. The height of 4 metres means that the tide will rise 4 metres above the figures shown on the chart, known as Chart

Datum. Unfortunately the level does not always fall to the chart figure. If you have a tide table which gives the height of *low tide* as well as high tide (Admiralty Tide Tables) it is easy. All that has to be done is to subtract the low water height from the high water height.

The result is called the 'range' and this is the distance that the level ranges up and down from low water to high water. Thus, if we found in this case that the range turned out to be 3 metres we would know that, since it is high tide, the level will fall 3 metres and that the low water level will be 3 metres from 5 metres – in other words, there will be 2 metres of water at low tide. There are ways of finding the range if Admiralty Tide Tables are not on hand, but enough is enough for the time being!

We must know what the range is if we are to be able to calculate how much the level will rise or fall above the low tide mark. Likewise we do not always anchor conveniently at high water. It may be half flood or three-quarters ebb.

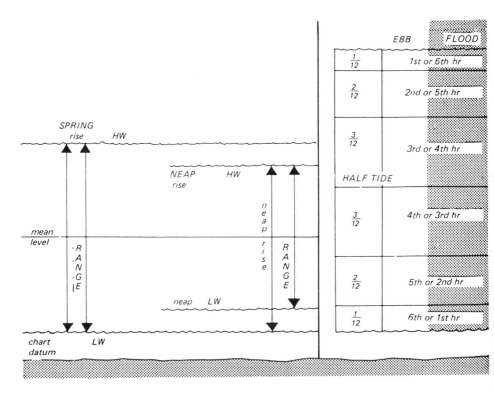

Fig 39 How the tides work. The mean spring rise is roughly equal to the extent that it 'ranges' up and down between low and high water. Neap tides neither rise as high nor fall as low, consequently they range up and down a shorter distance. The table on the right shows the 'twelfths' rule. The period is not quite a convenient 6 hours, but is about 6 hours 20 minutes on average.

Easiest of all is when we anchor at dead low water because we can see at once whether there is enough water to float in – if there is not, we go aground.

There is a very simple rule called the 'twelfths rule' for working out the amount of tide that will rise, or fall, above low water (Fig 39). We have seen how the level moves quickest around half tide, either flood or ebb. Now, in the first of six hours of ebb or flood the level moves roughly one-twelfth of the total range. It moves two-twelfths in the second hour, then three-twelfths in the third, three-twelfths in the fourth, two-twelfths in the fifth and one-twelfth in the sixth (six hours roughly from low water to high water). To be even rougher in our calculations we can say that the level rises to, or falls to, a quarter in the first two hours, half in three hours, and three-quarters in the fourth hour. The mate may never have to choose an anchorage, but will at least understand why the skipper sometimes delays mealtimes.

Reading the chart

The main difference between a map and a chart is that whereas a map concentrates detail upon features of land, the chart is concerned with coasts and seabeds – which is why only idiots attempt to use maps for navigation. Reading a chart consists of being able to look at the land and the chart and reconcile one with the other. It also means that you can study the chart when the land is out of sight and, assuming you know your whereabouts, visualize where you are going on the chart, how long you will take to get there, and what the seabed beneath you is like. You will know where to look on the horizon when land is expected, which lights and lighthouses you may expect to see, and so on. The important thing is to always have a 'feeling' of position on the chart as well as having a plotted position. This means that as you sit steering you will feel that land is just over *that* horizon in *that* direction and know at what angle the yacht is sailing relative to the coast, lightships, shipping lanes, and so on.

When the coast is in sight you will be able to glance at the chart and then at the land and identify which headland is coming into view. From this sort of chart reading you will then be able to look around and search for the buoys, prominent church towers, and so on, which according to the chart you should be able to see. In a small yacht the horizon is only just over three miles away at that low eye level, and low objects will not be visible until they have lifted clear of the horizon, but the chart will tell you in which direction to look.

Every chart has a compass rose on it which also shows 'magnetic' north. This is roughly the same north direction as the steering compass shows, and while I do not propose to go into detail here (it is an involved business) it is sufficient to remember that if you are steering west, for instance, and you note where the magnetic west on the chart is aimed, the yacht will be headed in that direction from wherever she happens to be on the chart.

Not every steering compass is accurate. Metalwork in the yacht and other influences drag the magnet of the compass out of proper alignment and this 'deviation' must be allowed for. It is the skipper's job to calculate the allowance, but it will explain why the course to steer may differ from the course drawn on the chart. For *rough* courses and bearings and assuming that the chart is a recent one (because magnetic north changes gradually over the years) it is possible to say that any course line drawn on the chart and then read off by transferring it to the magnetic part of the rose, with the parallel rules, can be steered by yacht's compass. However, this is such a generalization as to be heretical, and the result might be so inaccurate that your eventual landfall could be well out but, lacking a fuller knowledge of navigation, a rough heading taken this way would at least allow you to navigate *towards* help if some misfortune left you in charge of the ship. Ideally, a regular crew should set about learning simple navigation in greater detail.

The chart is a mass of information. The symbols show rocks, wrecks, buoys of different sorts, depths, shoals, deep channels, and so on. Many are self-explanatory, others less obvious. Each chart, like a map, is drawn to a particular scale which you must know before you can go much further. In terms of sea miles (slightly longer than land miles) you have only to look at the scale drawn on the *sides* of the sheet. This is Latitude. One minute of Latitude is one sea mile. The scale at the top and bottom of the chart is the Longitude and must not be used for measuring distance in miles.

Buoyage

Buoys serve as both signposts and warnings. Each has an identity such as a name or a number which can be checked against the chart, and at night most buoys show an identifying light signal which is also shown on the chart and listed in the nautical almanac. Buoys are also distinctive in colour, shape, and by the topmark carried. It might seem from the above that it would be almost impossible to mistake one buoy for another by night or by day, but this is by no means the case and here lies one of the prime mistakes made by yacht navigators.

Our first sight of a buoy is often at extreme distance and it is a mere speck without colour or shape; herein lies the warning. If we are expecting to see a particular buoy in a particular direction and at a particular time we tend to *take*

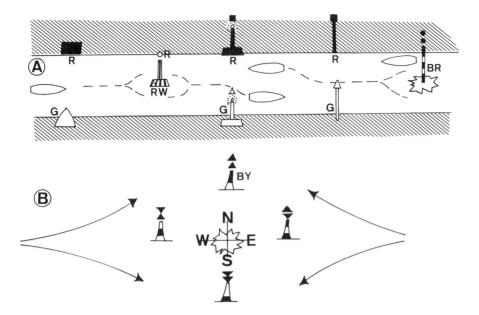

Fig 40 In (A) typical buoyage is shown. Note that the two vessels are passing each other by keeping to the starboard side of the channel. The IALA cardinal system in (B) is based upon indicating the safe side of a danger, and tall buoys have a black/yellow coding with black cones in pairs designating north, south, east or west. By night distinctive light sequences are shown.

it for granted. Even at night a distant flash too indistinct to identify properly might be assumed to be the buoy we are expecting and the boat navigated by it accordingly. This urge to take for granted must be the cause of literally hundreds of navigational accidents, not only to yachtsmen, but to other seamen down the centuries. So, be absolutely certain.

Fig 40(A) shows some of the more commonly used forms of buoyage. There are many others, but all serve the same purpose in showing the mariner where the safe water and where the dangers lie. In the main and in European waters a safe channel is indicated by placing green conical buoys on the starboard side and red can shaped buoys to port as *you go into a river*, or in the direction of the main tidal flood stream. Be very clear about this. You might enter a river leaving a particular buoy to port and upon leaving the next day again leave it to port and in doing so wreck the yacht. If the buoy is to be left to port on the way in it will be left to *starboard* on the way out, though this may feel wrong.

Buoyage also includes permanent fixed beacons, poles and other devices such as lighthouses, light floats and so on. At night light characteristics range widely from perhaps a fixed red light to rapid flickers and occulting lights which are on all the time but go out at regular intervals. I do not propose to go more deeply into the subject; suffice it to say that buoyage is important and needs to be studied in depth. However, I cannot omit reference to the all important Cardinal or IALA system shown in Fig 40(B).

When you see a black and yellow buoy with two black cones as a topmark, check (a) how the cones are arranged and (b) how the black and yellow areas are placed. Even if the buoy has a name painted on it which you cannot read you will be able to tell whether the buoy is on the north, the south, the east or the west side of a danger. These IALA buoys are in fact ringed around the danger; they are *outside* it. Having established which side they mark you can then judge where the danger lies.

The best way of remembering which is which is as follows:

Black cones points upwards, black areas on buoy upwards = UP NORTH; Black cones points downwards, black areas on buoy downwards = DOWN SOUTH; Black cones points together (looks like a bobbin) and with black in the middle = Bobbins wind wool = WEST; Black cones points apart and black top and bottom, no convenient mnemonic, except for being opposite = EAST

At night the lights are very distinctive being a series of rapid flashes. You can remember the north buoy because it is continuous; the east side buoy has groups of three quick bursts (the least of the four) so least is east. The west buoy with groups of nine is the most, so west is best. South with six bursts has no mnemonic.

Other buoys I should mention are 'safe water' buoys or marks and 'isolated danger' markers. The former are jolly with red and white vertical stripes and a red ball on top like lollipops. So remember they are fun and therefore safe and can be passed on either side. The isolated danger marks are gloomy with black and red horizontal bands and two black balls on top. Gloom and danger are associated, so keep clear.

Chart depths

One very important feature of the chart is its reference to depths. Colour tinting gives a first indication of whether the area you are looking at is in deep or shallower water, but the system of tinting may vary from one chart to another. An Admiralty chart, for instance, may show yellow for dry land, green for beach and shoal patches, blue for shallower water and plain white for deep water. Other charts published for yachtsmen may show white or green land areas, pale yellow or dark buff beach areas, white or pale blue for shallows and dark or pale blue for deep water. The clue in each case lies in the figures, the 'soundings' indicating depths. First, though, have a look at the printed information under the title. Today all British charts are metric, depths are in metres, but you may well come upon an old chart which is still based on fathoms.

You might find that depths vary from, for example, 40 metres in the deep water to 2.4 on a bank and perhaps 2.1 on a shoal which dries out at dead low water. An underlined figure means that the bank, shoal, rock, beach or whatever actually sticks up by that amount at the very lowest tides of all. The importance of being able to read the depths is realized when we are asked to take a look at the chart for the skipper who may be unable to leave the helm. A typical question might be: 'What water is there on the bank just west of so and so buoy?'

Make a habit of looking at the chart whenever you think of it. If a buoy is in sight, find it on the chart and consider where the yacht is in relation to it. Suppose the buoy is about a mile away on your port bow, about half-way between the bow and the broadside-on position. Look for the buoy on the chart, then look at the course you are sailing and picture an imaginary boat at the position which would allow it to have the buoy on a line between bow and beam (that broadside-on position). What you have done in effect is to take a bearing of your position by eye.

If two buoys are visible, one beyond the other, and they come into line with each other, you have only to draw a line on the chart through these buoys to know that the yacht must be somewhere on that line. This is a transit. If a buoy was absolutely dead ahead of the yacht and you glanced at the course she was steering you would have taken a compass or 'magnetic bearing' of the buoy – allowing for deviation of the compass being conveniently nil, of course. These sorts of navigational checks are the basis of coastwise pilotage. Buoys, churches, headlands, lightships and so on are identified on the chart and then used in one way or other as you sail along, and each contributes a little more to establishing exactly where you are on the chart. Combine this with study of the depth, allowance for tidal currents and the plotting of a course line from what you are actually able to steer according to where the wind is, and you have a good overall conception of what navigation is all about. You will soon take it a step further and begin using the hand bearing compass to take your own bearings.

The hand bearing compass is a little compass with a prism sight on it which is lined up with some object of navigational value, after which the bearing shown in the prism is read. There is a knack of using the compass in any kind of a seaway and it is worth practising. Having read off the bearing, perhaps 170 degrees, you then go to the chart, find the object of your bearing, and then lay the rules across the middle of the magnetic rose with the edge on 170. 'Walking' the rules across the chart until the edge is on the object and drawing a pencil line tells you that the yacht is somewhere on that line. Now, if you can find another identifiable object at roughly right angles to the first and take another bearing and plot it, the crossing of the pencil lines will be, in theory, where you are on the chart. Again there are small adjustments to be made to these bearings for complete accuracy. If it is possible to take a third object between the first two and repeat the process, there will be an intersection of pencil lines in the orm of a small triangle – a 'cocked hat'. The yacht will be somewhere in the

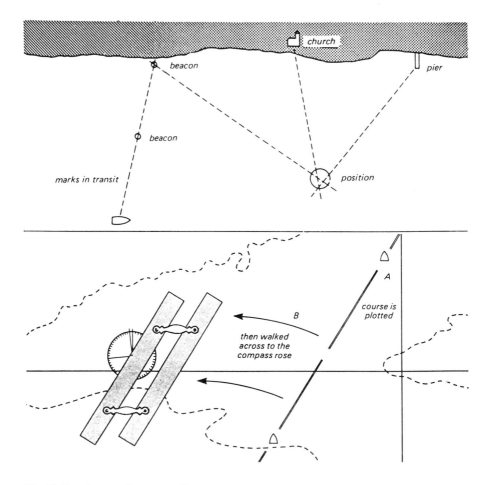

Fig 41 Bearings and courses. Shown here is a position line obtained by having two identifiable marks in line and a three-point fix by compass. The bottom sketch shows how a plotted course is transferred by means of parallel rules to the nearest compass rose on the chart so that its magnetic (or true) bearing can be read.

middle of it. The smallness of this hat is the measure of your care in taking the bearings (Fig 41).

From all this you can see how important it is to steer the best compass course possible or, if you have not been able to keep dead on course, to be able to tell the navigator your *average* course and what you think your error has been during the time you have been steering. A sensible skipper makes a point of being nice about it if the helmsman admits candidly that the course has not been dead on.

Steering by compass is a knack soon mastered, but it takes more than a knack to become a good helmsman. Too much tiller waving makes the yacht go slower. The aim is to sense each off-course swing and anticipate it by a gentle pressure of the tiller one way or the other. (See Steering by compass in Chapter 6.)

There are plenty of mates who take on the navigation entirely and prove better at it than the skipper – the latter happily relinquishing the job to them. This is a matter of personal choice, of course, but what is really important is that the mate should, in an emergency, be able to plot the yacht's position on the chart, even if it is only an approximation. Having VHF radio in a yacht is a valuable safety factor should assistance ever be needed, but it is not much use if you cannot tell your rescuers where you are.

Nowadays there are a variety of electronic position fixing aids such as Sat-Nav, Decca, Loran and so forth, and at the pressing of a few buttons these produce a Latitude and Longitude reading which can be plotted on the chart in

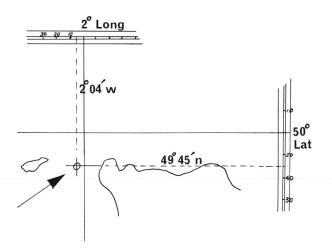

Fig 42 Plotting a Lat/Long position. A scale of longitude is found at the top and bottom of a chart and Latitude down the side margins. A Decca position of Lat. 49 degrees 45 minutes north and Long. 2 degrees 4 minutes west is plotted by ruling lines on the two readings and thus obtaining a 'cross' (shown arrowed).

seconds. We have a Decca system on board in common with thousands of other British yachts, and provided the basic navigation is kept up as well our Decca positions provide instant and accurate confirmation. Transferring the position shown by Decca to the chart is quite simple. It might, for instance, state that we are at Lat. 49 degrees 45 minutes North of Long. 2 degrees 4 minutes West. Using the Latitude scale on either the left or right edges of the chart we can measure and draw a line on the chart, roughly where we think we are at Lat. 49° 45′ and then from the scale of Longitude shown on the top or bottom of the chart, project a second line at Long. 2.4° West to cross the first line. (In the event of an emergency and a VHF request for our position we would not need to plot at all, but simply read what our instrument showed at the time.)

The shared decision

We spend our lives making decisions of one sort or another, from unimportant ones to major decisions affecting our lives. When cruising we are faced with an entirely new breed of problems so totally different from those met ashore that they constitute a fascinating challenge. Nevertheless they can be difficult to cope with, and two minds are often better than one. Although it is a skipper's job to cast the final vote, being responsible for the safety of the yacht and her crew, the mate can and indeed should discuss and influence the final decision.

Issues at stake might vary from whether to sail or stay in shelter; whether to anchor or to go to a marina; to make for one destination rather than another or whether it might be better to abandon the overall cruising itinerary as planned perhaps because of unsettled weather and agree on a much curtailed one. Such issues as these can be decided harmoniously in one boat or give rise to much friction and disappointment in another.

In order to be able to share decisions the mate must be in possession of all the facts relating to them; the weather situation, the safety of a particular anchorage, the suitability of boat and existing crew to cope with bad weather and so on. It is a skipper's job to decide when to reef sails, how much anchor cable to let out and when to start the engine, and no shared decisions are needed unless the mate is of equal experience and has useful alternatives to suggest.

The vital point to bear in mind is that we are cruising purely for pleasure and we do not *have* to go for this port or that, we do not *need* to make a grim effort to keep to an itinerary. In fact the aim should be to avoid unnecessary stress of all kinds. Of course it would be very dull if we never took an occasional gamble, stayed safely in harbour waiting for an ideal weather forecast, but on the other hand, we should never gamble without carefully considering all the facts.

A typical decision might involve a change of plan while at sea. The latest weather forecast may speak of a rapidly approaching depression and winds changing direction and strengthening. What had looked like being a quiet passage with a fair wind now promises to become a struggle with head winds and rough seas – nothing the boat and crew cannot cope with, but unpleasant and exhausting. The options might be: a) keep on, motoring hard before the weather turns nasty in the hope of getting to port before the deterioration sets in; b) turning round and going back, hopefully to get into shelter in time and c) altering course for another and closer port, one which perhaps you may not like very much. You debate the pros and cons, make a decision and act on it. The vital thing now though is that however it pans out the decision was a joint one, nobody is to be blamed if it is not the right one!

Never base a decision on what other people may choose to do in other boats. Your boat and your crew are a totally different matter. Every yacht has her limits in terms of what her crew can stand up to. Even a mate of only slight experience can help clarify a situation simply by listening to the alternatives with an open mind.

Handling dinghies

Dinghies are an essential part of cruising. If you plan to anchor the dinghy will be your only link with the shore, and unless you can handle one you will be dependent on others. Most cruisers carry an inflatable dinghy of some sort which can either be rowed or used with an outboard motor. If possible, learn to row in a conventional rigid dinghy because inflatables are not as easy to row in a straight line and a quicker, dipping stroke is needed.

The best way to learn is by choosing a windless day and a spot which is free from strong tidal currents, and simply splashing around until you get the knack of it. In fact a pleasure park boating lake is ideal. Do not pull hard when learning because you are bound to miss a stroke and 'catch a crab' (fall over backwards!). Undignified but otherwise harmless. Take small, gentle strokes at first, gradually lengthening them. Immerse only the oar blades and try to wedge a toe under the sternsheets (the rear seat) to stop you from 'catching a crab'. Concentrate on keeping a straight course. If the dinghy insists on turning, simply row an extra stroke on the side towards which she is turning or stop rowing and dip one oar blade in the water to slew her back. Practice is the best teacher.

In time you must learn to 'feather' the oar blades each time they return ready for the next stroke. This just means half twisting your wrists downwards so that

Children and dinghies are a natural pair; be sure that they learn to row properly, understand the dangers and wear lifejackets. It is also wise to teach them how to use an anchor.

the blades turn horizontally. When rowing against a stiff breeze this feathering technique greatly eases work and lessens wind resistance. You will need to know how to bring a dinghy alongside the yacht or a dock. When rowing an inflatable the bump does not matter much, but a rigid dinghy can do damage to a yacht's topsides.

When going alongside an anchored yacht always aim to end up with the dinghy pointing the same way as the yacht is lying. This is essential particularly if she is anchored in a strong current or a stiff breeze. Always end up facing the current in any case. The best approach is at an angle, aiming for the yacht at the point where her main rigging meets the deck. In a very strong current aim even further forward than this which will then allow for the dinghy being carried downstream while you are trying to catch hold of the rail. Row a little right up to the yacht and lift out the inner oar nearest the yacht at the last moment. There are better ways of going alongside, but these you will learn in due course.

As inflatables are rather hard work to row, and indeed almost impossible to row in strong wind or tide conditions, most people use an outboard motor. If you can manage your garden motor mower an outboard should be no trouble. Many have a clutch which means that the motor can be started and left out of gear until you are ready to move off, others are straight drive and once the engine is started you move. When you arrive at your destination you have to guess when to stop it! This comes with practice. Usually an outboard pushes you along at a fast walking speed, quite fast enough when learning. Keep an all-round lookout for other boats, which you will not hear over the noise of your motor. If it is choppy or if there is a heavy wash from passing boats slow down or you will swamp your own boat and soak your passengers. Try to avoid patches of floating weed, plastic and other rubbish which may jam your propeller, and make sure that your dinghy is 'trimmed' correctly. Trim means that when loaded with passengers the dinghy is floating evenly and with the bows very slightly higher than the stern.

Always wear a lifejacket, or at any rate do so if it is choppy and always after dark. Carry a torch also after dark plus a dinghy anchor. Never rely on the outboard entirely; always carry oars as well. Make sure you have a bailer of some sort and never allow people to stand up in a dinghy. The most dangerous time is when transferring between yacht and dinghy. (See Chapter 6, Crewing – Basics for first-timers.)

Remember the rise and fall of tide when going ashore; note where other dinghies have been left. A falling tide could otherwise leave your dinghy dangling by its painter or alternatively a rising tide could result in it being jammed under a dockside projection. In the case of an inflatable the safest course is to carry it well up out of reach of the tide and always secure the painter.

Maintenance

Although boats are built from waterproof materials the harmful effects of salt and weather are continually at work. Running repairs to rigging, sails and engine are usually carried out by the skipper, but there is plenty more to be done.

A regular hosing down on deck with fresh water followed by cleaning of glassfibre and a coat of Boat-wax or other polish both protects and beautifies as does the occasional cleaning of masts, booms, stainless steel fittings and so on. Accumulated pockets of grime soon become permanent stains, particularly on the hull just above the waterline where oil pollution is a major menace. Do not use harsh scourers which damage the gel-coat or shiny surfaces and keep an eye open for chips and scratches to the hull which should be filled with the appropriate resin putty before moisture can seep into the glassfibre laminate beneath the gel-coat.

The above refers to glassfibre yachts; the hulls and decks of wooden craft call for a totally different treatment. Potential deck leaks (rare in grp boats) are a source of trouble in many older wooden boats and can lead to serious outbreaks of fungal rot beneath them. Hulls also, if neglected, can quickly become rot infected in damp, airless areas below-decks. Wooden boats call for extensive attention to leaks where they exist, and a great deal of painting. However, many wooden yachts exist which are eighty or more years old; the potential life-span of grp hulls has yet to be discovered.

Many people prefer to leave teakwork, such as locker lids, coamings and the toe-rail along the edge of the deck as bare wood rather than varnish it, but much depends on where the boat is kept. If her permanent berth is down-wind of a big city or industrial area this bare teak soon becomes deeply ingrained with dirt. If it is to be kept bare it should be scrubbed at least once a month, preferably more often. Alternatively teak can be varnished or oiled. Varnishing is an annual job and in fact teak does not hold varnish very well. The wood must be bone dry and a succession of coats built up – at least four but more if possible. Never varnish flat surfaces which will be walked on unless either fine sand is sprinkled on the final coat while wet or non-slip adhesive strips are added afterwards. If the teak is to be oiled with teak-oil this is a messy business, especially if there is a wind blowing and, again, this must be done regularly.

Cockpit lockers easily become hell-holes into which just about everything is stuffed; turn them out regularly and tidy them because in an emergency such things as kedge anchor, boarding ladder or warps may be needed in a hurry and are liable to get buried or tangled.

Everything on board a boat which is meant to work *should* work and in particular this applies to the seacocks – the taps which shut off the holes in the hull such as the toilet inlet and outlet, sink and wash basin, engine cooling water and so on. Ideally, as mentioned before, these should be turned off after use especially when leaving the boat, but even if this is not always done these cocks must be turned now and again to ensure that they do not stiffen up. Some day it might be vital that a seacock works.

Below decks a regular fresh water wipe-over is essential because salt splashes and a salt atmosphere otherwise leaves the interior clammy, and clothing, bedding, books and so on soon suffer. Some items of equipment such as heaters, cookers and the like are not really salt-water proof and residual salt soon results in rust and corrosion which a fresh water wipe down and a light oiling can prevent.

On a sunny day it is good to open up lockers, turn mattresses on their sides and hang out sleeping bags (always lash them or they will blow away) and generally get the warm, dry air into every nook and cranny below. The boat will smell sweeter and any clamminess will be banished. It is very easy to collect a lot of unnecessary gear on board – so turn out the lockers regularly and take ashore anything not needed. Never leave dirty clothing on board, soiled tea towels etc. as these soon create a stale atmosphere, and whenever possible wash the oilskins in fresh water and give them a good airing on deck.

Answer to ship's light test in Fig 35: 1–B, 2–D, 3–A, and 4–C.

8 MARINAS

I must admit to being always a little edgy when we are approaching a marina that is new to us, you never know what to expect. If it is one you are familiar with you know exactly where to enter it and you can anticipate what is going to happen and what you will have to do as mate – but entering a strange marina can be hectic and nerves can become frayed.

No two marinas are the same. It may be that there are no difficulties and that the boat can be taken straight to the berth allocated and go in or alongside without fuss so that the mate has only to step ashore with lines. On the other hand you may have to look for a berth, perhaps to be turned away by the marina staff at the last moment and directed elsewhere, and then all manner of difficulties arise ending in the mate having to make a flying leap for the jetty.

Of course it is often possible to call up the marina staff on VHF radio and be given instructions on where to go and how to get there; or you may have a detailed plan of the marina in the pilot book. Much also depends upon how manoeuvrable the yacht is under engine and whether the day is calm or windy. A long-keeled yacht which needs a lot of room and engine for turning, and which cannot be steered in a straight line astern can become quite unmanageable in a fresh breeze. Conversely a fin-keeler, which is handy to manoeuvre ahead or astern, or a very quiet day pose few difficulties.

The approach can then be tense. The crew are alert for waving marina staff, searching for printed notices, trying to see if there are any empty berths which look like visitors' berths and the skipper meanwhile is trying to peer forward to avoid other manoeuvring yachts, maintaining enough steerage speed, but not too much in case the boat has to be stopped or turned.

Many marinas have clearly marked visitors' waiting berths where you lie pending specific instructions. This usually means going alongside other waiting yachts – not always so easy since such waiting berths are often close to the marina entrance in an exposed position where wind and waves make a gentle approach more difficult. Thus for the mate there can be a great deal of rushing from side to side with fenders as the boat is directed and re-directed to this berth or that. The warps at bow and stern may have to be rearranged, the skipper may be asking for directions as to the whereabouts of, for instance, 'berth 34, aisle D' or he may be having all sorts of problems in turning the boat around in a confined space.

All the above may sound discouraging, or maybe I am painting a blacker picture than necessary. The more experienced one becomes in entering marinas the better accustomed one is to sizing up what is needed in a particular set of circumstances.

Types of marina

Marinas built within harbours can be entered at any state of tide, day or night. They are likely to be sheltered from most winds and unaffected by tidal streams, although subject to tidal rise and fall. Half-tide marinas which cannot be entered or left once the tide level has fallen below the cill are fairly common. The cill is a sort of low wall across the entrance which maintains a lake of sufficient depth during the hours of low tide. There are river marinas which may be swept by tidal currents on flood and ebb; coastal marinas protected by massive walls, the entrances to which may become very rough in strong onshore winds; and there are locked-in marinas, access to which is by a pair of huge gates which are only opened for perhaps one hour either side of high tide. Once inside there are no currents, little rise and fall of level and complete security.

Both the locked-in and the half-tide marinas have one major disadvantage. During the busy part of the summer, the main holiday months, there is a vast amount of yacht traffic, consequently the opening of the locks or the rise of tide to a level which gives access to the half-tide cill tend to mean a mad rush of boats which have been waiting either to leave or to enter. In some marinas this rush is carefully controlled by the harbour staff. Yachts are held back to allow the exodus to take place and then the new arrivals are directed to vacant berths one at a time. Others are not so well organized and it almost becomes a race to find a place inside. Tempers become frayed and not infrequently there are a few bumps. From all this you can see that it helps to know what to expect in the different types of marinas.

The mate in action

The mate's job during the approach to a marina for the first time is a multipart one. The skipper may leave the steering to the mate (see notes on handling under power later in this chapter) so that the pilot book instructions can be studied and the lie of the land identified on the chart. Or he may prefer to leave this research to the mate. At a fairly early stage sails will come down and motoring will begin. Just *when* depends upon whether the approach is in sheltered water – there is not much point in struggling to furl sails out in rough water when the boat will be entering sheltered water minutes later.

During the entry the skipper will want to have an unrestricted view ahead, so if the crew are running around hanging out fenders and placing ropes in position they will be very unpopular; better to do this as soon as the boat stops rolling around. Fenders should be tied to the guardrails and laid on the side decks in readiness, and the bow and stern lines should be coiled, one end made fast and the other, plus the coil, passed out under the guardrail and back over the top ready for use. Having done all this, it is best to go back aft and stand behind the helmsman and assume a watching role.

There is plenty to look out for. Never assume that the helmsman has noticed the fisherman's marker buoy dead ahead or that the steamer backing out of a dock inside the harbour has been spotted. You will also be able to keep an eye open for notice boards, waving marina staff and exiting yachts.

The correct placing of fenders and smart handling of ropes are vital. If you *know* the boat is going to be berthed port side to a jetty you will also know that

Approaching the pier with fenders correctly slung. In such calm and windless conditions there should be no problem.

four fenders will be needed on that side, two spaced about six feet apart at the widest part of the boat and just clear of the water and the others forward and aft of these – not right at the bow and stern because almost all yacht hulls slope away steeply at these points and the fenders would hang uselessly in space. Keep at least one other spare fender ready to jamb in where it may be needed in case of trouble.

On this a point of warning. Even small yachts moving quite slowly constitute an almost unstoppable force. If you see that the boat is going to arrive with a bit of a bump do not try to fend her off by hand or by foot – you will not stop her and you could risk injury. Jamb an extra fender in at that spot and hope for the best. It may be that the helmsman fails to stop the yacht in time and the bow pulpit looks like making contact with the stern of the boat berthed ahead. Once again do not try to check her headway by hand or foot. Having said all that, most arrivals alongside are gentle and orderly.

The mate's immediate concern when coming alongside is to get ashore with a line. According to the nature of the berth and the direction and strength of the wind – and the quality of the skipper's manoeuvre – the helmsman may want the bow or the stern line ashore first. If no such demand is made it is usual to step ashore with the bow line and, having made this fast, the helmsman will either jump ashore with the stern line or hand it to the mate to secure. Let us asssume that we are making a normal approach and that the mate is at the bow to take that line ashore. The line, as mentioned earlier, is secured to the foredeck cleat and the coil passed out through the bow fairlead and taken outside all rigging. It is held by the mate who will be standing *outside* the guardrails at the widest part of the boat, near the main shrouds. Holding on to these shrouds with one hand, the coil in the other and with one foot firmly on the side deck you are ready to step ashore – rather in the manner of someone waiting for a bus to slow down before stepping off the platform. Never jump. Wait for the gap between boat and jetty to narrow sufficiently to step ashore otherwise there is a risk of slipping and falling and this could be dangerous.

Once ashore, if the boat is still moving ahead despite the engine trying to pull her astern, the bow line will be used to check her headway. This means it will have to be taken to a cleat or bollard on the jetty somewhere level with the stern of the yacht – and this will have to be done quickly. Here use a technique known as 'taking a turn'. As you may well imagine, with the boat moving forward the line attached to her bow is also moving forward so the mate quickly winds it round the cleat or bollard one full turn and simply hangs on. To attempt to make any sort of knot would take too long *and* it could be dangerous to fingers which might get trapped in the line just as the weight of the boat is taken on it. By allowing the line to surge a little under load the weight is eased off gradually.

Fig 43 Never attempt to jump across the gap when going alongside; take up a
position as shown here with one foot securely on the rail but *outside* the rigging and
guardrail stanchions and one hand holding on to a shroud wire. With the coiled bow
line in your free hand wait until you can drop lightly to the jetty in safety.

Having stopped the boat the line is taken off the bollard and carried forward
of the yacht's bow to the correct cleat on the jetty and made fast. If the
helmsman has not already come ashore with the stern line this will have to be
dealt with quickly and attached to the jetty some way astern of the yacht. She is
now secured by a head and stern line and there is breathing space before
completing the adjustment with springs to guard against surging (see Fig 31),
final spacing of fenders, etc.

Marina berths and general layout consist of fairly broad approach channels
flanked by long planked walkways and small finger piers or jetties projecting at
right angles to them. Between each pair of finger piers there is generally room
for two yachts to berth, each lying alongside a finger. These finger piers,
however, do not extend for much more than three-quarters of the length of the
average cruiser, neither is there more than a few feet of space between
neighbouring yachts (Fig. 44). Usually getting a boat into one of these finger
pier slots calls for a tight turn and quick burst of engine astern to stop her dead
before she rams the walkway. In the previous paragraph we looked at the use of
a bow line to stop a boat's forward movement, as might be the case when going
alongside a dock or long jetty. When berthing by a finger pier the mate's job is
still to nip ashore with lines, but as to which line is made fast first depends on the
wind direction at the time.

Let us suppose that we are lucky, and in order to turn out of the main channel
into the finger pier we have to turn our bows dead into the wind. This means
that the wind tends to stop us and it will not have any ill effects on the steering

as might be the case if it was blowing us sideways against either the finger pier or the other neighbouring yacht. However, this head wind also means that the bows of our boat will have to be secured pretty quickly once she has stopped otherwise she will begin to blow backwards again. Once the bow line is on, though, there should be no more trouble.

Entering such a berth with a fierce beam wind is often extremely difficult for the helmsman, and the mate must be ready to take whatever action may be needed. For instance, if the wind is trying to push the boat bodily sideways away from a finger pier the odds are that her bows will go first – which means hitching the bow line to any cleat as quickly as possible, then hurrying aft to grab a stern line before the stern blows away from the pier too. The likelihood is that the helmsman will have had to enter the slot in a crab-wise manner because of the wind, so you can see that nobody quite knows which end of the boat is likely to need attention first until she is alongside.

The worst of all approaches is when the wind is blowing directly into the slot. It then becomes extremely difficult to stop the boat under engine astern and

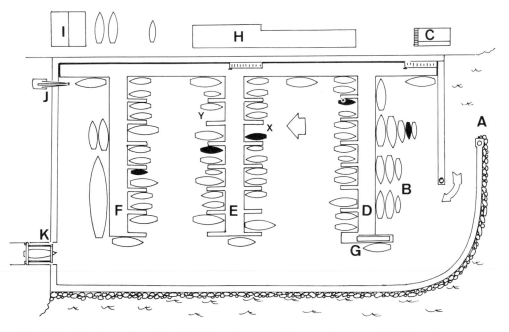

Fig 44 A typical small marina. (A) The entrance with protective arm. (B) Visitors' berths. (C) Marina office and control (D,E,F,) Pontoons flanked by finger pier berths. (G) Fuel berth. (H) Showers, toilets, shop etc. (I) Repair shed. (J) Mobile crane. (K) Travel hoist. For a new arrival in a fresh breeze berth (X) might prove tricky to enter, whereas berth (Y), being a head-to-wind approach, would be easier.

inevitably there is a tendency for her to slew sideways. This is when quick, intelligent crew work can redeem a tricky situation.

As stated earlier, though, the majority of entries into berths are quiet and successful – more often than not with the aid of some helpful fellow yachtsman ashore waiting to take lines.

On any approach to a marina berth the mate will be on the foredeck ready with the line. It is best to stand dead in front of the mast for as long as possible so that the helmsman's view is not obscured. Being forward and with a much higher eye-level than the helmsman the mate also gets a much clearer view of things and is more likely to spot any vacant berths before the helmsman sees them. Here it is best to point at the berth, since the helmsman would be highly unlikely to hear a shout over the sound of the engine.

Lock gates

With half-tide marinas where there may be a mad rush to get in, this can be avoided by hanging back and going in last, hoping that there will be a berth

Entering a crowded marina this mate has knelt down so that she is not obscuring the skipper's view. She has her warp ready coiled and she is on the lookout for a vacant berth.

available. With lock gates it is sometimes different. Usually the gates remain open during the hours either side of high water and after the first rush one can come and go without panic. But sometimes, locks are 'worked' – as for instance when they form the termination of a canal upon which the marina is situated. This means that with an almost unlimited supply of water from a canal, which is higher than the average sea level outside, a vessel can enter the lock, the gate is closed behind her and she rises to canal level as water is admitted to the lock via sluices. When leaving things work in reverse; the lower gate is closed, the level rises, the upper gate opens then closes behind her and down she goes to sea level as water is drained out of the lock.

Because lock keepers do not like wasting water they will wait until a number of craft have entered the lock before operating the gates and sluices. Let us imagine that we are approaching an open lock gate from the sea. Inside it and moored to the walls there may already be a number of yachts, fishing boats and even larger vessels. A lock keeper may direct us to a position, perhaps by a wall, maybe alongside another yacht. He may even ask for our lines to be thrown to him (see reference to heaving lines in Chapter 6) or there may be vertical wires or bars on the walls of the lock to which our lines may be secured. We will, of course, have our fenders in position because they will certainly be needed. Perhaps on both sides.

Our lines must be doubled back to the bow and stern – this is vital. As the water level rises or falls in the lock the tension of the lines will need constant adjustment. In some cases sliding rings are provided on the walls so that our lines can slide up or down, but even these can jam. By doubling back our lines it also means that we can 'slip' them whenever we need. We must also remember that if our lines have been passed through rings higher up the walls, as might be the case before going down, it will not do to bring them aboard via the fairleads (which means *under* the guardrails) if our lines will shortly be leading sharply upwards as the boat descends. To do so, in fact, could mean that the whole strain would be pulling upwards against the wires. Both bow and stern lines must be manned and adjusted continually – and there is a hidden danger here. Quite often, having entered and made fast there comes a long wait while other vessels are trickling in. The temptation is to leave the lines un-watched, perhaps to brew a cup of tea; then the gates close slowly and noiselessly and suddenly the water level is falling quite unnoticed. It can so easily happen. Suddenly there is a wrenching noise as cleats pull out of decks, ropes part as guardrails are torn out. Remember also that in a few locks the rush of water from sluices as they fill can bang a boat against the wall. Be wary also if the lock is a free-for-all and not properly supervised because there will be a rush to leave and a great deal of propeller wash. Those spare fenders may be required!

Handling under engine

Some boats are quite easy to manoeuvre under engine only; others much less so, particularly if there is a fresh breeze blowing. In either case it is useful for a mate to know the basics of boat handling under engine, even though it may never be necessary to take over. A mate who knows the difficulties can then anticipate problems brewing and take steps to minimize them.

A typical cruiser deprived of steerage way tends to drift broadside to the wind and gradually turn her stern into the wind. She weathercocks; bows downwind, stern upwind. When manoeuvring under engine in a stiff breeze this tendency has either to be overcome or used to advantage. Boats with long keels,

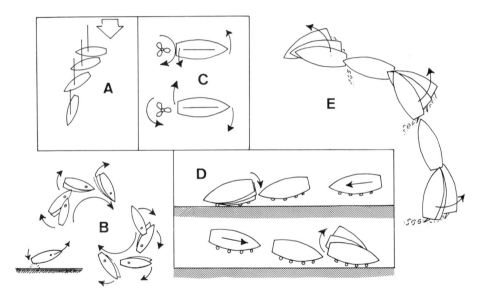

Fig 45 (A) A drifting yacht will typically 'weathercock' her stern into the wind. (B) Under engine a boat pivots her stern outwards when going ahead in a tight turn, but when turning stern first it is her bows which pivot outwards. When trying to motor away from a jetty, therefore, the outward pivot of her stern prevents the yacht from getting clear if she is turned too sharply. (C) Propellers tend to have a paddlewheel effect. A clockwise turning (righthanded) propeller when driving ahead tends to thrust the stern to starboard and the bows to port. The opposite effect happens when going astern with the propeller in reverse. In (D) the top diagram shows how this can aid a yacht which is going alongside a jetty portside-to. As the engine is put into reverse the propeller nudges the stern to port, thus making it easier to lay her alongside. In the bottom diagram going starboardside-to, the reversed propeller nudges the stern outwards away from the jetty. (E) Burst-turning. With rudder fully over the engine is given a series of short, hard bursts of power which have the effect of nudging the stern round without much forward movement.

high bows, or a lot of rigging forward of the mast to catch the wind tend to weathercock more than boats with short fin keels or less windage forward (Fig 45A).

Another common factor is the way in which boats behave when put into a tight turn ahead. When the rudder is put hard over, the stern is forced aside and the boat pivots as if a giant hand was holding the mast causing the stern to swing outwards. When the boat is moving stern-first, however, it is her bow which swings out as she is turned and she pivots around a point which is roughly in the middle of the cockpit. What all this means in practice is that you cannot make a sharp turn if there is not room for bow or stern to swing outwards, as might be the case if you were alongside a jetty and trying to steer away from it (Fig 45B).

Another common feature of boats under engine – it varies a lot from boat to boat – is the effect that the propeller has on steering. On the one hand it drives the boat forwards or backwards according to which way it is turning, but it also tends to paddle the stern sideways a little. You can see this happening if you let go of the tiller while motoring along; the boat will begin to curve away from her straight course. Most propellers turn in a clockwise direction when going ahead (viewed from behind that is) and this tends to paddle the stern to starboard. Remember: clockwise or right-handed propeller, stern to the right. The effect is opposite when going astern; propeller kicking left, stern kicking left. As with the weathercocking tendency it can be either a handicap or an aid when manoeuvring (Fig 45C).

Weathercocking, stern swing and propeller paddling are all influences when trying to put a boat alongside, and a good skipper bears them in mind if there is a choice of where the boat is to be berthed. For instance, if a boat has a strong paddle effect and a right-handed (clockwise) propeller (i.e., her stern will slew to port or the left as soon as the engine is reversed to stop her as she nudges alongside), it is easier to choose a berth where her *port* side will be against the jetty because she will then slew her stern *towards* it as she comes to a stop. If she was put starboard side to the jetty her stern would slew away from it as she stopped. Combine this with a strong breeze blowing off the jetty and she would soon end up with her stern swinging further and further out because her bows might be held by the bow rope while the stern was still free to swing downwind (Fig 45D). Being aware of such tendencies means that a mate can assess what is needed, hurriedly taking a stern line perhaps, anticipating orders, shifting fenders, and so on.

I know of some boats in which the mate does all the engine manoeuvring. Be this as it may (and it is a matter for individual agreement) the mate should be able to carry out straightforward manoeuvres such as approaching a mooring or anchorage, going alongside a fuel or water berth and so on. Control of speed is important in such cases. A boat will usually turn in a tighter circle on full rudder when she has plenty of power on, but of course if the circle has been misjudged and there is not quite enough room it means that you will hit something that much harder. Avoid such fast turns if possible. It is often better to go very slowly and turn the boat in a series of sharp full-power bursts. This means that with the boat barely crawling ahead the helm is put hard over and the engine opened up to full power for maybe three seconds then closed again. This utilizes the propeller paddle effect to the full and boosts the stern sideways without pushing the boat ahead too much (Fig 45E).

Knowing your own boat is important. Knowing that she will turn much more tightly to port for instance, that she can be steered dead astern in a straight line if needed or that she is very vulnerable to windage, influences every handling decision you make.

Marina living

It is usually much nicer when a yacht is berthed in a marina with her bows inwards against the finger pier, pointing to the walkway, because of the greater privacy this offers. With the stern to the walkway and bows pointing out, passers by can stare straight into the cockpit and cabin. The exception is when a stiff breeze is blowing. It is then far more comfortable with the bows facing the wind, thus sheltering the open companionway. In practical terms, though, once the boat has been berthed the effort of reversing her is not even considered!

Yacht crews seem to have an unwritten law about each other's privacy, which is rigorously observed by all except perhaps small children. It is also a law which extends (as a rule) to quietude. Now and then there's a party in the cockpit or a late night jollification aboard a boat but one takes it in good spirit. More irritating is the crew who play a radio loudly in the cockpit. With some large power boats the almost constant running of generators and warming up of powerful engines can be a great nuisance and many marinas forbid or restrict it. Just as annoying in the case of sailing craft is the clattering and rapping of rigging against the metal mast.

One of the mate's first jobs, having tied up, is to silence the rigging. The most effective way is to take every halliard and lead it right away from the mast. The main halliard can be led down to the side deck and secured, genoa and spinnaker halliards led forward to the bow pulpit and so forth. The topping lift may be in use but then a swifter or crane line can be used to silence it. This is a short cord secured to one of the main shrouds and used to pull the halliard outwards from contact with the mast. Whether berthed in a marina or lying solitary at anchor this silencing is essential to our own comfort too because below decks such rapping and tapping can become unbearable.

Most marinas provide shore amenities, toilets, showers, perhaps laundry facilities, also fresh water and (for those with current adaptors) mains electricity. Access to fresh water usually means there will be a coil of hose pipe at intervals along the walkways, although in some cases it is left to the user to provide the hosepipe. It is wise to carry a short piece of hose and suitable adaptors for attaching to the taps to simplify topping up water supplies. When watering a boat, during hot weather in particular, there are certain rules to observe. A coiled hose standing in hot sun can become a breeding ground for certain microbes which, while not necessarily harmful to health, can taint the yacht's water tanks.

The rule for watering, therefore, is first to run the water to waste until it no longer feels warm. If possible it is no bad thing to detach the hose from the tap and pour about a pint of water purifying solution through it before filling your tanks. Thereafter fill the tanks slowly to avoid airlocks – particularly so in the case of flexible plastic water tanks, which can be burst by filling under pressure. Having finished watering leave the hose neatly coiled for the next user, and never allow the end to fall into the dock which may be heavily polluted.

Rafting up

At the height of a busy season when there are more boats than berths available visiting yachts may be rafted up. This means that the yachts lie one alongside another, sometimes as many as six or even eight deep, each with fenders out on both sides, and moored together each with a bow and stern line carried ashore. The latter detail is important. Although these lines from each boat to the shore or walkway are not always very effective due to their length and narrow angle, the fact that they are there at all is a token of good seamanship. It is not considered good manners to hang on to another boat like a parasite allowing his lines to hold both boats (Fig 46).

Yachts may be rafted alongside a jetty or walkway, rafted between piles out in the river, or between mooring buoys – in some cases to a single mooring buoy. In each case the boat must be moored by her own lines and *then* secured to her neighbour. Since yachts will be leaving or arriving at intervals this insistence on the use of one's own lines can become vital. A raft of yachts lying in a tideway obviously needs a good deal more mooring care than a raft inside a tideless marina. If one yacht in the middle of such a batch of boats wants to

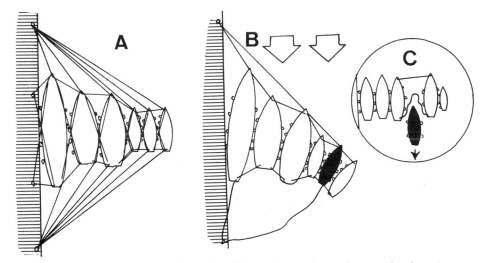

Fig 46 Rafting up. In (A) note that all craft have bow and stern lines to the shore but in (B) only two of them have their lines ashore, with the result that the whole raft sags away downwind. The inset (C) shows how one yacht leaves from the centre of the raft having made quite sure that the rest of the raft cannot break apart.

leave, a great deal of adjustment of ropes is necessary. The skippers of neighbouring boats must be alert to the risk of damage and, of course, any assistance they can give to the yacht leaving is greatly appreciated. Afterwards there will be a great deal of retying of warps to deal with.

Privacy in a raft is limited since cockpits tend to be parallel with each other. There is also the constant toing and froing of people from outer boats trying to get ashore. You might have to clamber over eight or nine guardrails in a large raft, but another unwritten rule is that in order to respect the privacy of others you must cross each yacht via its foredeck, *never* across the cockpit. It goes without saying, too, that you tread lightly – especially if returning late at night.

The procedure for going alongside a raft is much like going alongside anything else; fenders out and lines ready. It is good manners to ask the owners of the boat you are making for if they mind you coming alongside. Perhaps having been directed there in the first place by the harbour master this may sound fussy, but it is a friendly gesture to make. Sometimes, perhaps, the other boat may be about to leave anyway.

More often than not those aboard her will invite you to throw your bow line across. Do not be tempted to try too soon; the line will most probably fall short and have to be re-coiled and heaved a second time. Wait until the gap closes and you know you can get the line across, then toss it over accurately and lightly – do not hurl it at somebody's head. Ask the person who takes the line to make it fast and then you can begin to haul it in.

As the boats come together look aloft to check that the two masts are not going to entangle at their crosstrees. Very often the crews of both boats will line their respective rails with fenders and both boats will be heeled towards each other. Remember that even minor damage done aloft can result in the loss of a mast at a later date. A small kink in an alloy crosstree, a knock out of alignment; either is enough to be serious. A raft-up in a river is also prey to trouble if wind against tide conditions cause waves to develop. The rafted yachts begin to roll against each other and damage aloft is then almost certain. If you have to raft up in this way and you go ashore to shop, do not be gone too long if you do not know the conditions.

Another pitfall of rafting when there is a cross-tidal current to contend with is the tendency for the whole raft to be carried sideways despite all the lines tethering the outside boats to the shore. Such rafts are all very fine for a brief stay in fine weather, but again do not stray too far from your boat.

9 COPING WITH EMERGENCIES
In general

It is nowadays possible to buy a great variety of equipment designed for use in emergencies, most of it for use *after trouble has started*. Boats do not invite danger; they are no more potential risk than, say, caravans and far less risk than a car in which much of the risk lies in the behaviour of other drivers. In a boat most of the potential dangers are avoidable. Avoiding them is a matter of foresight, wise planning, good boat maintenance and common sense.

Fire

Any boat built of wood or plastics will burn fiercely and give off dense clouds of fumes if even a small accidental fire gets out of hand. The speed at which the serious fire can gain a hold is astonishing, and should a fire in a yacht reach this stage *it is probably unstoppable*. Only instant action with adequate equipment can prevent this from happening, so we have to think in terms of fire suppressing and escape.

Fires in boats can start in a variety of ways, apart from the obvious result of a careless cigarette smoker. A flare-up of a paraffin cooking stove, a cabin heater, an over-heated engine, faulty electric wiring or loose terminals (a very common cause), the explosive fumes from an over-charging battery, spontaneous combustion caused by a bundle of oil rags left in an unventilated locker, fumes from petrol and other highly combustible fluids ignited by a stray spark and, of course, that most lethal of all, the bottled gas explosion. Some risks are obvious to all, such as a fire from a chip pan (not to be recommended on boats) and the folly of someone smoking while petrol is being poured into the outboard motor nearby, but others are totally unexpected.

Warning devices such as engine overheating alarms, smoke detectors, gas detectors down in the bilges where gas might accumulate, and gas pressure alarms which indicate a loss of pressure and therefore a leak somewhere are all valuable, but they do not replace common sense and an alert crew. A gas alarm, for instance, must be suspended so deep in the bilge space to detect early accumulations of gas that its sensor is likely to be splashed by bilge water and instantly rendered useless. I would not be without our gas sniffer, but I still reckon my own nose to be superior.

Rigid rules for the use of gas, as mentioned in Chapter 4, plus correctly installed equipment, properly maintained, is the only sure protection. The regular replacement and inspection of electrical wiring (it is worth paying an expert to do this), the ventilation of the battery box, the clearing of all highly flammable liquids such as paints, spirits and the like from lockers, strict rules about smoking and, as mentioned in Chapter 4, strict procedure for using the cooker are all matters of basic care and common sense.

Although new rules concerning yacht building and flammable material are shortly to be introduced by the International Standards Organisation (becoming effective in 1992) the majority of yachts at present are equipped with foam filled mattresses which are highly flammable and productive of dense toxic smoke and fumes. A great many yachts also have a foam fabric covering to sides and deckhead which, once alight, creates a 'flame tunnel' of fireball intensity. Ideally we ought to replace all such foam with safe alternatives (BS 7176 and 7177) but of course this is impractical in most cases.

How then can we fight an outbreak of fire and prevent its spread? I must urge readers to seek specialized, detailed information from their local fire officer, insurance company, Boatbuilders Federation or other appropriate body. The following is merely a digest of such information.

There are several different types of fire extinguisher. The general purpose dry powder with a controllable nozzle; foam, also general purpose; the now largely superseded carbon dioxide; the Halon gas type (BCF and BTM); plain water of course, and the fire blanket. Of these the Halon gas is perhaps the cleanest and most effective, but it is now found to be ozone-destroying and consequently environmentally unfriendly. Powder and foam are very messy – which means that people may hesitate to use them during the first vital seconds after discovering a fire. Water, unless you have a pressure hose, is difficult to use and since it would require opening up, say, an engine box and thereby increase air flow in order to hurl a bucket, maybe risky too. The fireblanket is highly effective on a cooker fire, but only provided it is not held off the burning pan by the rails round the cooker.

How you actually fight a fire is dependent on speed of attack, accessibility without opening up enclosed areas, and having a large enough extinguisher to cope with both putting out the flames and *cooling the area afterwards*. A dry powder or foam extinguisher must not be smaller than 2 kg mounted in a prominent place and professionally checked at frequent intervals. Please do seek additional information.

Escape

One of the most likely areas for a fire to break out is by the main companionway where the engine and galley are usually sited. Make absolutely sure that there is easy exit from the forehatch, provided with steps if necessary. If you have a cabin skylight consider this too as a possible escape route. Could you get out by standing on the table? If the yacht has an after cabin, perhaps reached by means of a narrow alleyway near the companionway steps, it could be especially at risk in case of fire or if the boat was sinking. Has it a skylight or alternative escape route?

In a fire the restriction of draught and airflow is essential. Get everybody on deck, but close hatches behind them. Those on deck should instantly begin either launching the dinghy or preparing the liferaft for launching. More on this later in the chapter (see calling for assistance and abandoning ship).

Man overboard

Man overboard is an ever present and dreadful danger, but it need never arise. There is always a *reason* for someone falling overboard; strictly speaking it is not an accident. Carelessness, over-familiarity, and failure to observe sensible precautions are the causes. It is possible to be washed overboard in heavy weather of the worst sort, but not *lost* overboard providing sensible seamanlike precautions have been taken.

Guardrails, lifejackets and safety harnesses are the main safety factors, plus care at all times. Forget the idea that danger only exists in heavy weather; this is simply not true. It *always* exists. Nobody advocates wearing lifejackets or flotation garments night and day in calm, serene weather, nor is it necessary to wear safety harnesses, but at these times and especially at night one takes special care not to be lulled into a sense of false security.

The unguarded moment is the real danger; forgetting to hook an arm round a stay perhaps when standing up to use the binoculars, using two hands to work while standing straddle-legged on the foredeck, scrambling round the spray-hood without hanging on, even changing places in the cockpit in rough weather with the boat heeling steeply. In fact more people have been lost from cockpits and their illusion of safety than from foredecks.

Usually the skipper will decide when safety equipment must be worn. At night, in the dinghy, in choppy weather or in bad conditions at sea there might be an order 'jackets on – safety harness on'. It will probably be a rule in fog, when there is shipping about, and in any other emergency or simply as a precaution for the non swimmer. At other times it is probably a matter of personal choice. Some people prefer to wear some form of buoyancy equipment all the time when they are afloat, others only when the conditions are rough – what is important is that no one should feel embarrassed if they are the only one wearing safety gear or hooked on with a safety harness. The various types of lifejackets and buoyancy aids and the essential differences between the two are described more fully in Chapter 12.

Children should always wear lifejackets and/or safety harnesses. They will want to move around and to climb because this is their nature, and a pair of stout wires secured along the deck full length proves an anchorage for harness hooks which allows them to roam freely in fine weather.

Of course it is better not to fall overboard in the first place and the safety harness is designed with this in mind. If there is a reluctance to wear both harness and jacket (and on top of oilskins and sweaters this adds up to an untidy and restrictive bundle) the harness should be first choice at night and in rough weather, or at any time when finding and picking up a person is likely to be difficult. More important than anything is to see that the harness is hooked on to the boat. The only exception to this rule is if there is any chance of the yacht sinking or being sunk – in fog among steamers say. The hook rope may be ten feet long with a midway second hook. Never use the full length unless it is needed as scope for working on deck, unnecessary slack rope means that you have further to fall if you should slip. Hook up short and stay hooked up. If you want to move, unhook and hook on again at once.

A person falling overboard at night is at even greater risk and at least one lifebuoy should have an automatic flashing light and a whistle attached to it. Of equal importance by both day and night is the Dan-buoy. This is a six foot flag staff which has a float and a counter weight to make it stay upright. The staff is as thin as a fishing rod and banded with reflective tape and orange fluorescent paint or tape so that the staff and its orange flag can be seen clearly; at night any powerful torch can pick it up vividly at a hundred yards or more. Some Dan-buoys also have their own flashing light. You can imagine that in anything like rough water a person in a lifebuoy will be lost from view between the waves for much of the time, whereas a flag staff is seldom lost to sight. Remember though that unless the Dan-buoy is released quickly when somebody falls overboard it will be quite some way away from them. Other equipment should include a spare lifebuoy and a throwing line.

A Dan-buoy, having a weight below it, does not drift much even in a strong wind, but lifebuoys certainly do drift – being light and highly buoyant; for this reason each should have a drogue. This is really a small parachute of about two feet diameter and made of fairly heavy synthetic material so that it will sink and in doing so will act as a drag. Drogues are quite easy to make and attached to one of the lifebuoy lines and rolled up neatly they work automatically. Lacking a drogue the wind would whip a lifebuoy out of the casualty's reach in a second.

The pick-up

There is a great deal of difference between a fully crewed boat and one in which a lone woman is left to cope with the rescue of her partner or skipper. We will look at her problem first and assume that she can handle the yacht competently, although perhaps not with the skill of an experienced single-handed sailor.

First she must get a lifebuoy into his hands so that he can stay afloat. She may do this by sailing the boat back to him and dropping it as she sails by. Wild throws are a waste of time and in any case the wind could well blow a buoy out of reach before it can be grabbed. She must release the Dan-buoy, keep her head and try to do one of several things. She may try the expert's approach of getting down-wind of the man and then luffing the boat head to wind so that the boat shakes the wind out of the sails and stops just alongside him. Unless she is confident of bringing this off it is best not attempted. An easier method is to sail back to him on any course, except one which is dead before the wind (unlikely in any case) and as she draws near, ease out all the sails to slow the boat until she is close enough to throw a line to him. She must let the sails go completely and leave the boat to look after itself while she helps the man in the water to pull himself alongside. This second method is not fool-proof. Under certain conditions the boat will stop, go astern, bear away, sail a little then stop again, and so on, and the man in the water will be dragged along with her.

She might also, if she knew how, hastily lower the sails, start the engine and motor back to him indifferent to wind and sailing. There are two huge dangers. Hastily lowered sails may mean ropes over the side and the possibility of a rope getting round the propeller. This would put the yacht out of action and allow it to drift further and further away from the man in the water. The other danger is the spinning propeller, which could inflict dreadful injuries. It must be a hard and fast rule that the engine (not just the propeller) is stopped when going alongside anyone in the water. A merely declutched engine may still allow 'propeller creep'.

If the yacht has a roller jib the task is greatly eased; the sail can be got out of

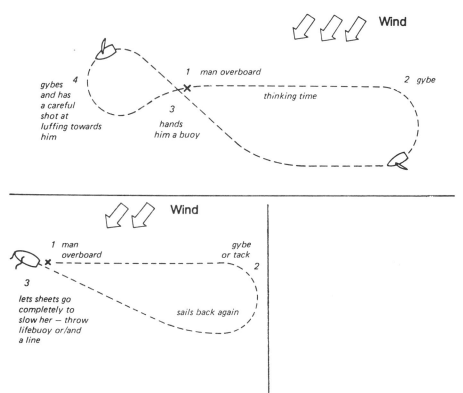

Fig 47 Man overboard. This manoeuvre is not the usual one suggested; it is modified to suit the less expert helmsman. The aim is to get a lifebuoy into the swimmer's hands first, thus giving the helmsman a little more time in which to think and act. Arrows represent wind direction. The second example is an operation which the very inexpert might attempt. If she can get the boat back close to the man in the water, lying across the wind, and let the sails flap completely to slow the yacht, she might then get a line to him.

the way quickly and with little risk of ropes over the side. Under mainsail and engine the yacht can be manoeuvred easily provided she is kept more or less head to wind and the mainsheet can either be hardened in tightly or allowed a bit of slack as occasion demands. This simple tactic of returning to place a lifebuoy into the casualty's hands gives the rescuer time to overcome panic before attempting more difficult manoeuvres. It buys time and it is easy to remember. The all-important thing, however, is to *stay close by*. The Dan-buoy marker will indicate the approximate area of the casualty but you will need to be able to see him before you can hope to bring the boat to a standstill within arm's reach. Now let us look at the problem as a fully crewed yacht might deal with it.

In this (simulated) rescue the lone mate has sailed back to the casualty, freed the sheets to slow the boat, and lobbed a lifebuoy right into his hands. She now has time to think and to prepare for the pick-up.

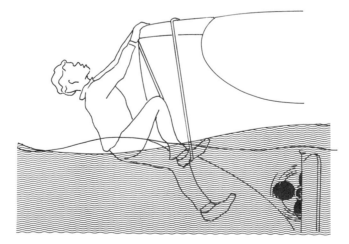

Fig 48 Although it makes good sense for an unskilled person to make the pick-up attempt under engine, and the loop of line over the side is a great help to the tired casualty, beware the danger of the propeller. Feet and legs tend to swing underneath the curve of the hull. Cut the engine completely and/or rig the loop further forward.

Opinion about the ideal manoeuvre to adopt is always changing. Should you gybe at once; should you put the boat on a broad reach, noting the course heading so that you can return on the opposite broad reach for the pick-up; should you simply bring the boat to a crash stop, drop headsail and start the engine? The value of any drill is that it takes over when your mind becomes blank. Only two things really matter. (a) That you appoint someone to watch the casualty and point constantly to him and (b) that you get the boat back quickly but under control and make the final approach from down-wind. How this is done does not matter so much.

In any man-overboard rescue situation the boat must be under control though, otherwise you may get back to the casualty only to find that you cannot manoeuvre the boat or cannot stop her from sailing ahead. As long as you do not lose sight of the person in the water moments spent getting the boat under control are an investment. Remember to reassure the casualty though; let him know rescue is at hand.

Getting the casualty aboard

Assuming that the casualty has been able to grab a thrown line – by no means a certainty if chilled or exhausted – the rescuer's whole aim must now be to get a rope round him, knotted securely under the armpits. DO NOT leave a casualty hanging on to the rail by his hands while you are busy doing other things; a rope supports the head and shoulders clear of the water and guards against his being swept away.

For any couple sailing as a pair I strongly advise that the inflatable dinghy is kept on deck during a passage half inflated, if feasible. It can be launched (tied on of course) next to the casualty so that he can drag himself into it. In its half inflated state it is relatively simple even for a tired person to get at least half-way aboard it, and once again you have *bought time*. This advice applies equally to fully crewed boats, especially those with high topsides. Another alternative is to rig a loop of rope over the side into which the casualty can get his feet. If this loop is deep enough under water for him to do this, however, it means that his feet and legs will tend to drift underneath the yacht and if the propeller is turning this can constitute a danger (Fig 48).

We also have to remember that the person in the water will be weighed down by sodden clothing, he may be shocked and perhaps bitterly cold and unable to make much physical effort; so what can be done?

If there are two guardrail wires the lower one should be secured at the end by means of a lashing which can be cut – or have some form of slip-hook. If this

Lifting on the main halliard. Only if the halliard winch is sufficiently powerful is this method practicable. Some idea of the deadweight of a soaked and inert adult can be seen from this picture.

wire cannot be released it will severely hinder any attempt to roll the casualty aboard over the edge of the deck. The same applies to canvas spray dodgers. Can they be released? Further forward the side-deck may be too narrow for a rescuer to exert much strength.

A lone woman, quite frankly, has little hope of rescuing an exhausted male who cannot do much to help himself. Her hope then must be to secure him to the side of the boat and put out an urgent MAYDAY call at once. This may sound a forlorn hope but in fact there are a number of cases on record where lives have been saved in this way. (Procedure for sending MAYDAY distress signals is explained later in this chapter.)

For a more numerous crew and in a larger yacht the mainsail halliard is a favourite recommendation, but the mast winch is then powerful enough for the job which it certainly may not be in a yacht of about 30 foot length or under. We have tried this method and found that I cannot lift my husband even when he is dry and standing on deck. Do not consider this method as a viable one unless you have *tried* it. There is a workable modification however.

You need a pair of blocks, each with two sheaves (wheels) and made up into a tackle. Rather like the mainsheet in fact. This needs a lot of rope because when fully extended the blocks must be a good twelve feet apart. This tackle will give

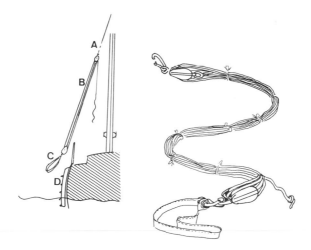

Fig 49 Perhaps the only way in which a heavy person in wet clothing can be hauled out of the water, if the halliard winches lack the necessary power, is by hoisting aloft a powerful tackle (B) on the main halliard (A). A webbing sling (C) can be passed over the casualty's shoulders, and if there is time to rig the boarding ladder (D) the casualty may be able to help himself a little. The tackle is kept in its fully extended state ready for instant use and lashings of wool or some other easily snapped thread keep the rope parts from becoming tangled.

you a four-to-one power, and by hoisting it a little way on the main halliard you then have a means of lifting a heavy weight out of the water and up to the height of the rail. If this is not powerful enough use a triple and a double block with the treble one at the top; this gives 5:1 power. This tackle must be ready for instant use, which means fully extended. So that it will not get tangled up in stowing it, tie some thin bits of knitting wool around the swatch of rope parts at intervals (Fig 49).

We also have a collapsible ladder, weighted at the bottom rung to make it sink well under water, but be wary of ladders because they are very difficult to climb when you are actually in the water. A point of warning here. Many owners boast of the permanent ladders fixed to the sterns of their boats. 'Ready for instant use' they tell us. These may be fine for bathing, but just imagine a boat which is pitching heavily as she lies stopped head to wind to rescue somebody. That ladder may then become a lethal battleaxe plunging down on the head of any swimmer who gets too close. At best it will be wrenched out of his grasp as the yacht's stern swoops upwards; only if there is no swell or the

Fig 50 The fixed stern ladders of many yachts are not always a safe means of rescue from the water. If the yacht is stopped head-to-wind and plunging, her stern ladder will become lethal to a person in the water. Only in calm seas or with the yacht lying beam-on and rolling rather than pitching should the stern ladder be used.

boat is lying beam-on to the waves is a stern ladder a practical means of recovery (Fig 50).

Obviously it would be sensible to try out some of these rescue methods, wearing a lifejacket of course, or maybe when enjoying a gentle swim over the side when there is no risk of anything going wrong. Also try a few sailing manoeuvres, perhaps 'rescuing' a lifebuoy thrown overboard for the purpose with everybody taking turns at sailing the boat. No matter how proficient you may become at this, though, do remember that it is *nothing remotely like the real thing.*

For the mate, however, practice at manoeuvring is all-important. We can learn to sail, learn how to get the best out of the boat and become a competent helmsman or woman, but to manoeuvre at slow speed in a fresh breeze is very different. Go for an afternoon's sail and 'play' with the boat. Try easing off the sheets and slowing the boat to a mere crawl, try letting her stop dead with sails shaking then get her going again. Find something in the water such as a small mooring buoy or some floating rubbish and try bringing the boat to a standstill alongside it. Find out what the boat has to teach you. Not only is it great fun, but someday it might be the difference between life and death.

Keeping things in perspective

I agree that this is not a cheerful chapter – just a necessary one. I could just as easily write a similar chapter about camping detailing the dangers of thunder storms, poisonous mushrooms and fierce bulls. By identifying the risks in any sport or situation we go a long way to eliminating them.

Nowadays everybody, including young children, knows that if we should need help in any sort of emergency we reach for the phone, dial 999 and ask for the type of assistance required. We may never have to do this but it is comforting to know that help is there for the asking. Boats are no different. The huge majority of us go all our lives without having to ask for help, but it is essential to know how to summon it.

Until fairly recently we had to rely on distress rockets and flares or using flag signals or just waving frantically, but nowadays we have VHF radio. Admittedly there are people who call for help when it is not really necessary – or should not be. Things like running out of fuel when they could sail home; feeling seasick; believing they are sinking because the toilet is over-flowing are typical examples. Even in such cases as these the ever patient Coastguard will still advise and reassure, and perhaps direct a nearby fishing boat to stand by.

More serious cases might include genuine illness or injury aboard, serious

A half inflated dinghy carried on deck offers great advantages in terms of rescue. An exhausted swimmer can sprawl into the deflated end in the water and rest while preparations to get him aboard are being made.

damage, crew exhaustion and bad weather brewing, uncertainty of position in potentially dangerous waters, stranding on a sand bank or a rock in open waters and so on. There are various degrees of distress call depending upon the degree of danger and risk to life.

Ideally the mate will take the very simple examination required to become a bona fide VHF operator, but even the mate who does not hold the certificate should at least know how to operate the radio and request assistance. It is the skipper's duty to demonstrate this. The nub of the operating technique is the microphone. Held in the hand it has a speak button, and unless this is pressed while speaking those receiving the call will not be able to hear your words. Thus it is *press to speak, release to listen*. An easy way to master this simple but vital technique is to take a small torch and pretend it is a microphone; flash-speak, off-listen. Either enlist a friend to help or practise in front of a mirror.

There is a laid down procedure for sending distress calls but the essentials are as follows. If it is plainly a life and death situation or rapidly becoming one, call 'MAYDAY, MAYDAY, MAYDAY' followed by your yacht's name repeated three times. Then WHERE YOU ARE, WHAT IS WRONG, the sort of HELP NEEDED, a description of your BOAT, and the number of PEOPLE ON BOARD. The call might sound like this: MAYDAY three times; YACHT JANE three times; TWO

MILES SOUTH RAMS HEAD; SINKING QUICKLY; NEED IMMEDIATE HELP; THIRTY FOOT BLUE SAILING CRUISER; TWO PEOPLE ABOARD; NO LIFE-RAFT; OVER. This is the sort of information needed to mount a rescue by helicopter or lifeboat, or by any other boat nearby. If it is not quite in that order it does not matter, but if you do not give enough information time is wasted if the coastguard has to ask for it. Remember: name, where, what is wrong, help needed, people on board and what the yacht looks like. If the skipper (who may be incapacitated) has previously filed a passage plan with the coastguard, details of your boat will be on record on the computer.

Not all urgent situations are *distress* ones meriting MAYDAY calls. If there is no *imminent* danger and *immediate* assistance is not needed the urgency PAN PAN signal is used and it has priority over all traffic other than distress calls. The procedure is: PAN PAN (three times); HELLO ALL STATIONS (three times); THIS IS (name of yacht three times); then position, nature of urgency, assistance needed and invitation to reply and acknowledge. Examples of a PAN PAN might include engine failure at a critical position, running aground in a potentially dangerous situation, dismasting etc.

If the urgency is a medical one a PAN PAN MEDICO call is used (see Chapter 13). There is also the SECURITE call (say-cure-e-tay) used for warnings of a navigational nature or for a warning of immediate bad weather. An example might be the sighting of a dangerous baulk of timber, a navigational buoy adrift or suchlike. The call ends with an instruction to switch to a particular working channel.

All the above calls are broadcast on the distress frequency Channel 16 (or 2182 kHz MF) thereafter shifting to a working channel, with the exception of MAYDAY which is made and continued on the distress frequency.

Abandon ship

Everybody on board should have some knowledge of the procedure for abandoning ship, how the liferaft is operated and how to send the distress call. Should a liferaft be used, make every effort to enter it without getting wet. The real danger is the risk of a deep chill or hypothermia should you be in the raft for some hours, and for this reason sleeping bags and other warm items should be grabbed. In a well-run yacht a 'panic bag' will be carried containing food, water, distress flares, ship's documents, and so on. All should wear lifejackets. Unless the yacht is sinking rapidly the raft should be kept tied on and ready to cut free from the yacht. The yacht, of course, will be much easier for rescuers to spot than a small liferaft would be.

Lifeboat and helicopter

When the lifeboat arrives on the scene her coxswain takes charge. He may decide to take the yacht's crew aboard the lifeboat; he may simply put one of his men aboard to take charge, or he may decide to take the crippled yacht in tow. You can assist by getting the sails down and making sure there are no stray ropes in the water to entangle with the lifeboat's propellers. Everybody must wear a lifejacket and do exactly as instructed. If a helicopter arrives it may be difficult to lower a crewman on your deck because of the yacht's mast and rigging, but again get the sails down. You may be told to jump overboard so that you can be picked up from the water. *Wear your lifejacket*, keep calm and obey instructions.

Rockets and flares

Despite the fact that VHF radio is now a first line of defence in an emergency a mate should also know how to use distress signals. To begin with they should be kept in a clearly visible place on board, somewhere dry and accessible. Read the instructions at least once at the start of the season, check whether they are still in date – if not pester until they are replaced.

Rockets are handheld and send a cluster of red stars high in the air. Flares are also handheld and burn with a bright red light. There is also a yellow smoke flare for daylight use. The value of distress signals is two-fold. One, to draw attention and two, to guide rescuers to the scene. Just because you have VHF radio does not make them obsolete. They are a vital second string.

10 PROVISIONING

Aboard small cruising boats the cook depends on fresh provisions to a large extent, but for all that she might well have to call on the ship's stores from time to time. Whether the boat is used for day sailing, weekend or more extended cruising – or as a floating caravan in harbour – she should be equipped with basic stores as well as a completely separate emergency stock. Here is a suggested list of basic stores to start the stock list rolling. Quantities, of course, depend on the number of crew, the amount of locker space available and the length of cruises planned.

Tea	Jam	Rice
Coffee	Marmalade	Fruit drinks
Sugar	Dried and vacuum	Tinned meat
Dried milk	packed meals	,, fish
Long-life milk	Crispbread	,, stews
Salt	Cracker biscuits	,, milk
Pepper	Sweet biscuits	,, vegetables
Sauces	Porridge oats	,, puddings
Chocolate	Packaged soups	,, soups
Cooking oil		,, fruit
		,, beer

These form the absolute basic, non-perishable stores; some items kept against real emergencies, others used regularly and replaced as they run out. Such things as crispbread, a couple of tins each of, say, stew, soup, milk, beans, rice and fruit should be kept in a separate locker and left intact for a real emergency. The wise cook will include matches and will stow these items in one of the less commonly used lockers – probably in a sealed box and well away from the normal stores.

Incidentally, if possible choose imprinted tins, or otherwise devise some method of marking them before removing the labels. It may sound unnecessary, but labels left on tins, especially those stowed in the bilges or lockers which can get damp, gradually disappear. They can clog up the bilge pump; but almost as bad, a meal of rice pudding, fish and Irish stew could easily result! So, mark the tins and keep details of the different markings safely.

Make a list of all the basic and emergency food stores and note any items used so that they can be replaced at regular intervals. In addition it is a good idea to add to the list such things as washing up liquid, paper towels, cleaning powder, matches, toilet paper etc. This means that when the time comes for restocking they will not be overlooked.

Whether you are planning for a short passage or a long cruise it is a good idea to work out a rough menu. This does not necessarily have to be kept to religiously, but it will help with the victualling and is a basic on which to work. It is a good thing to take account of the weather outlook when planning the menu. Obviously if there has been a long, fine, warm spell and it looks like continuing, it is possible to include more salads and be a bit more ambitious with the meals. On the other hand, in unsettled weather it is best to cater accordingly and include quickly prepared meals and things which can be eaten hot or cold.

The sort of meals the cook can produce at sea depends upon the cooking equipment available. It is very rare to find a boat with only one burner nowadays where the cook has to juggle to produce even the most simple meal. Two burners; two burners and grill; two burners, grill and oven are much more common, allowing the cook to produce progressively more complicated meals. Add to the equipment an ice box or a fridge and, if the sea conditions permit, there is the wherewithal to produce 'home' type meals.

What is important is that meals and hot drinks appear at regular intervals. This is particularly important when sailing at night. The long hours on watch appear much shorter if hot drinks (soup, bovril, cocoa, coffee etc.) appear from time to time. If a tuck box with chocolate, biscuits, nuts, and fruit is on hand this also helps.

Early morning at sea after a long, hard, cold night can catch people at their lowest ebb, and this is the time when something hot and filling and simple to prepare is needed. Instant porridge oats is an easy answer and never fails even among the squeamish.

With the wide selection of tinned, frozen, vacuum-packed and dried meals available, producing a variety of meals on board is relatively simple provided the conditions are reasonable and the cook has found his or her sea-legs. One point worth noting, food does not have to be hot to be nourishing. If conditions are really bad something in the order of a hunk of bread and cheese and an apple would serve quite well.

In any case cooking in a seaway is not really as difficult as it sounds. The old adage 'you get used to anything in time' applies to sailing, and gradually as the stomach settles down the motion of the boat is taken in its stride and the cook really begins to enjoy the challenge of cooking at sea.

11 SAILING WITH CHILDREN

The sailing mother who takes her children afloat must be capable of taking full charge of them on deck and below. The skipper will be fully occupied with the sailing and seamanship side, particularly when under way. The mother must see that the children are properly dressed for the various passages and that orders are followed implicitly. In fact, it will be up to her to ensure that the skipper is free from worry and able to give all his concentration to sailing so that there are none of those sudden panics and alarms which all too easily dismay and frighten children who do not appreciate what they are all about.

Apart from the question of inflexible feeding times, toilet arrangements, etc., tiny children can be safely tucked into carrycots and present no problems. At the other end of the scale, children of around eight upwards, used to boats and the sea, can become useful members of the crew, providing their interest can be kept alive. It is the in-betweens – the crawlers, the toddlers, the questers – who present the greatest problems. This is the age when children begin to copy, when they show eagerness to help with all the jobs on board; let them, and select some of the more simple tasks such as brushing the cockpit, 'coiling' a sheet, polishing winches etc., which they can handle by themselves.

So long as sailing is not thrust down their throats to the exclusion of everything else, children brought up on the family cruiser in a happy atmosphere take it all in their stride. This is the time when some careful thought about the type of sailing most likely to attract really young children is needed. Children are easily frightened and in any case they quickly become bored, so the wise skipper will not undertake any prolonged passages until they are used to the sea, confident in the ability of the parents and boat to cope with whatever might arise, and settled into a sailing routine.

All this takes time, of course, and parents who are looking ahead to years of happy family participation in the sport should be patient and spend the first weeks, months, maybe even season, on short picnic cruises with plenty of trips ashore, swimming, fishing, exploring, etc. The occasional night away or longer passage can be fitted in if the weather is good and settled. With proper ground-work, patience will be rewarded, and without much lost time a happy well-trained family crew will be embarking on longer cruises, well fitted to cope with longer sea passages and looking forward to the adventure of *real* family cruising.

From the very beginning a child has to learn what is right aboard a boat and what is wrong. The lesson of complete and immediate obedience must also be put across, but from the very start explain the whys and wherefores of the rules. Give a practical demonstration of why the mainsheet must be kept clear; why the head must be kept down when gybing and going about; why there is only one way to step aboard a dinghy. A practical demonstration of these points and any others that spring to mind, although painful, is the surest guarantee of obedience I know. Go a stage further and turn the dinghy over (choose a nice warm day and shallow water) and try out man-overboard drill too. There is no better way of getting the message across, but do not make a tense frightening fuss about it. Above all make sailing fun for all the family and if at some stage the keenness of one or more of the crew seems to be waning, leave them ashore with relatives while the rest of the family go. So long as they are not forced to join in they will soon feel they are missing out on the family fun and show eagerness to join in again.

On a calm day with a nice working breeze and when you are going nowhere in particular let the children take over completely and practise a few manoeuvres unaided. There is no better way of learning, but keep an eye open for other craft nearby.

Just as the saying goes that a man needs an extra foot of boat for every year of age, so it is said that the duration of a sail should be in strict relationship to age, certainly as far as children are concerned. Obviously a keen ten year old could put up with quite a long passage, but down the scale a five-hour passage for a fiive year old (unless part of the time is spent asleep) is more than enough, and it is very rare for a child of this age to remain interested for such a period.

Children's safety

The safety of their children is probably the greatest worry for sailing parents, and although the dangers afloat always seem much worse than shore-side dangers, in actual fact so long as the rules are observed children are considerably safer at sea than they are playing at home, crossing roads, etc. The first rule, of course, is obedience; immediate obedience to all commands, and this must be instinctive. There is no doubt that a disobedient child afloat is in continual danger, and unless willing obedience can be taught everyone on board will be in a constant state of tension.

The wearing of lifejackets must be automatic. Before a child steps into a boat of any sort – dinghy tender, launch, cruiser, what-have-you – the jacket must go on. Here parents can do a great deal to help. As mentioned earlier, children love to copy, so the whole business of lifejackets should be something shared by all the family – part of the 'dressing up' prior to going afloat, in fact. This is just as important for older children whether they can swim or not, although later on as the swimming child becomes more used to sailing the rule can be relaxed somewhat in quieter weather and at anchor or on moorings.

The cockpit and the cabin are obviously the places for children when sailing, and when in the cockpit small children should always wear a safety harness – again even at anchor or on moorings. Sooner or later the adventurous child will go overboard, but so long as a lifejacket and/or safety harness is worn and there is a dinghy handy, there should be no difficulty at all in getting them back again quickly and easily. Equally important, whenever a child is in the cockpit or on deck an adult should always be around to keep an eye on them.

Really small babies are rarely seasick – in fact they enjoy the motion of the boat – but older children are just as susceptible to motion sickness as adults. This is another reason why longer passages should only be undertaken when children have become used to sailing and coping with seasickness when it happens. Treat seasickness as perfectly normal, but do not discuss it too much in front of children. Sleep is the best cure for seasick children, so give them one of the sleep-inducing tablets and tuck them in below. Ten to one they will wake up refreshed, hungry and quite fit again.

Clothes for children afloat

Keeping children warm and dry is vitally important. There is a good selection of tough sailing clothing available for children and miniatures of many of the grown-up models to be found. Like adults, children should have plenty of warm clothes to wear underneath their wind and weatherproof suits, and these suits should be big enough to take all the extra clothes worn underneath and to allow for growing. They should be chosen for ease of putting on and taking off and the jacket, or smock, should have a hood to protect the head and neck against wind and water. A good hat which comes well down over the ears is a good bet for the cold, miserable rainless days and the child should have a towel scarf for the neck, good woollen gloves, socks and – an absolute must – proper non-slip deck shoes. A sun hat which protects the head and the eyes from glare is essential for summer sailing as well as a lightweight anorak for keeping out the cool summer breezes. Needless to say, one complete change of clothes is essential.

Lifejackets and buoyancy aids

Most of the manufacturers of safety aids produce lifejackets and buoyancy aids for children, and in really small sizes too. Basically the difference between the lifejacket and the buoyancy aid is that whereas the lifejacket is designed to float an unconscious body in the water in the correct position, face upwards with the head well supported, the buoyancy aid will only give *assistance* to a person in the water, thus ensuring that no effort is needed to keep afloat. The important point is that the buoyancy aid will not necessarily float an unconscious body the right way up as will the lifejacket.

Consult the manufacturers for the most suitable garments for your particular needs. Perhaps the best solution would be a lifejacket for non-swimmers and a buoyancy aid for swimmers? However, for children try on several different models. If they feel happy and comfortable in them they will be much more likely to wear them happily as a matter of course. Remember the child will have to wear the jacket for hours on end so comfort and freedom of movement are vital considerations. Incidentally, some jackets and buoyancy aids for children are available with built-in safety harnesses.

Safety harnesses

Safety harnesses are also available in really small sizes. Again make sure the

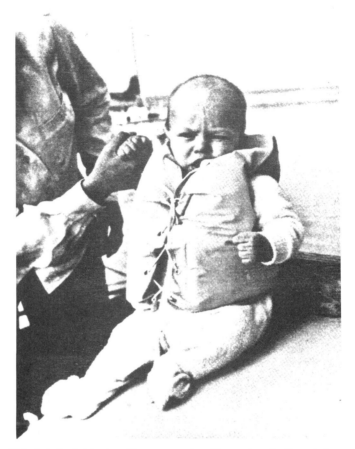

There are lifejackets for babies too. Never, never buy bigger sizes for them to 'grow into'. Lifejackets must fit snugly or they are dangerous. They can easily be sold later on.

child is happy and comfortable in the model chosen, but this time pay just as much attention to ease in putting them on and taking them off. Some harnesses are very complex and difficult to sort out quickly when time is short. Do not forget that there should be good, strong attachments in the cockpit for harnesses and perhaps one or two down below, as well as an attachment line all along the deck. To begin with put small children on short lines until they find their sea-legs and lengthen the scope as they become more used to life afloat and what they can and cannot do. The importance of safety harnesses cannot be over stressed – they are vital if sailing parents are going to have any peace of mind at all.

Coping with children in their various age groups

BABIES

Luckily the carrycot acts as pram, cot, play-pen, the lot, and solves a good many problems when taking babies afloat. The main problem is finding safe stowage for the cot below and in the cockpit when sailing. It should be wedged in securely on a bunk down below to stop it sliding around, and you should choose a place where there is some fresh air but no danger of the occasional dollop of spray. Secure fastening in the cockpit is not quite so easy, but by means of chocks and rope lashing it is possible to fix the cot so that it stays put. Preferably it should be fixed amidships, with the baby lying fore and aft, otherwise the cot will have to be moved each time the boat is tacked. Disposable nappies, ready prepared baby foods and milk make looking after the small baby a simple matter, and a plastic bowl makes a good bath.

Unlike older children, babies do not need amusing, but they do need careful watching. Remember the glare from the water is particularly strong, so do not expose the tiny baby to too much sun afloat. Remember, too, that sea breezes are drying and they can also be very chilling.

CRAWLERS AND TODDLERS

There is no problem about sleeping accommodation for the slightly bigger child. They take to bunks very rapidly, and in fact two small children can be tucked into one bunk (not a quarter berth of course) with no trouble at all. Naturally tiny children will need a bunk canvas or board to keep them secure. In any case, whether there is a bunk canvas or not it is a good idea to wedge them in thoroughly with cushions so that they do not roll around as the boat moves. There are specially small sleeping bags available, but since children grow quickly this is not altogether a practical idea. Perhaps a duvet tucked well in would be useful here?

Small children, unless they are particularly nervous, sleep through almost anything afloat, so if any longer passages are envisaged it is often a good idea to make them at night when the small ones are asleep below. The snag about this is that when the crew are feeling tired after an all-night vigil, healthily refreshed children are wide awake ready for the start of a new day. At this stage amusement is needed and a good supply of toys. Choose floating dolls and animals for preference and books which are expendable. Include one or two teaching toys which can be played with on the cockpit or cabin floors. Children in this group must wear lifejackets at all times when out of their bunks and safety harnesses in the cockpit and on deck.

Toilet arrangements at this stage are simple. No child minds missing out on a

A lot of concentration goes into hoisting the club burgee. Having learned to tie a few knots children enjoy finding uses for them.

bath for a day or two and potting with a plastic pot should present no difficulties.

FOURS TO EIGHTS

The age of curiosity and copying. Provided children wear lifejackets at all times and harnesses when venturing into the cockpit and on deck they should be allowed to help with the simple tasks – washing down decks (with an adult to draw up the water), hoisting and lowering flags, etc., and given a spell at the helm, if they show the inclination. Start teaching them simple knots, begin swimming lessons, and if they are learning to swim ashore give them as much practice as possible during the weekends. Learning to swim in a pool is one thing, but children should start getting used to swimming in wavelets and in tidal conditions as soon as possible.

If they show interest take time to explain what is happening, why a thing is done a certain way. Let them see you sticking to the rules they are expected to keep. Naturally there will be times of boredom and amusements will be needed. Get some educational books on the sea, buoys, flags, sea birds, boats of various classes, etc., so that they can do their own spotting. Puzzles, card games and books are a must, and a cheap fishing line is also an asset when it comes to keeping children occupied while sailing. A towing toy of some sort also helps too.

Fit in plenty of trips ashore, picnicking, fishing, bathing, and on these trips begin rowing lessons if children are interested. But right from the start teach proper dinghy routine, getting on board, behaviour on board, and leaving the dinghy.

Sleeping arrangements are just the same as for smaller children, with older children occupying a whole bunk if space permits. Teach them the proper routine with the marine toilet, show them how it works, explain why knobs are turned and so on. Taking in the information gradually like this, as equipment is used, they soon acquire a good all-round knowledge of the routine afloat.

OVER EIGHTS

Children of eight and upwards who are used to boats can be really useful on board. Those introduced to sailing more recently can be just as useful provided they are allowed to join in and help right from the start. Trust them to help with the various jobs, as this way they will learn in double-quick time. Once again the lifejacket is a must in the cockpit as is the safety harness on deck, especially when sailing. This is the age of the why and wherefore, but however much curiosity a child shows the golden rule holds good – instant obedience to orders.

Again arrange lots of shoreside trips, bathing, exploring, etc., and have plenty

Deck scrubbing is an ideal excuse for playing with water, but never allow children to draw up water in the bucket while under way – the drag could easily pull them overboard.

of books on board. Teach knots, splices, whippings and the principles of sailing, and above all let the child of this age discover the dinghy. Then, having learned how to row, let them venture off alone on trips ashore. Naturally a child, however capable in a dinghy, must wear a lifejacket. Once the child has gained confidence in the dinghy a great stride has been made. In fact many children consider dinghy duties as their own special perks, taking over the trips ashore and the journeys back and forth with gear and provisions as their own jobs, thus relieving the older members of the crew of at least one chore. What is important is that by learning how to handle the dinghy properly the child has assimilated a tremendous amount of basic seamanship – allowing for wind and tide when tying up alongside or making for the shore, right of way rules, etc. This is particularly the case when children start to use the outboard motor on the dinghy. In fact these are the first lessons in potted seamanship which once learned will never be forgotten.

Remember, though, that even at this age boredom soon sets in, so never expect too much in the way of long-term interest. Always have some alternatives up your sleeve and keep the food as interesting as possible. Appetites will be hearty, and at times of boredom meals will be the highlights of the day. Above all let children help down below and in the galley if the deckside chores lose interest. Who knows, you may not have a top-notch deckhand in your crew, but you may well have a first-rate sea cook.

Do's and don'ts for children afloat

• Never let small children copy father and try to draw water from over the side. The sudden tug as the bucket fills, whether large or small, could easily pull them overboard. This is just as important in harbour as at sea. The tide on some coasts is sometimes sufficient in itself to give a hard enough pull to catch a child unawares.

• Never allow children to swim from a boat unless there is someone on deck to watch them, a dinghy in the water and a ladder rigged to help them on board again. Anyone who has tried to get even a very light person on board from the water will confirm how difficult this can be. In any case, a child should never be encouraged to swim from a boat, except at fairly slack tide. The tide is usually stronger than you think.

• Never allow children to climb around on deck unless there is someone watching them all the time. When they do, make them abide by the standard rule for yachtsmen – *a hand for yourself and one for the ship*. Once this becomes instinctive children are halfway to becoming seamen. It is a rule that applies to grown-ups too.

• Keep to the rules about wearing lifejackets and safety harnesses scrupulously so that they become automatic. A point to stress: a safety harness is useless unless it is hooked to a stay or hook. This must also become automatic.

• Make it a rule for children to wear waterproofs every time they go on deck at sea. A dry, warm child can enjoy the thrill of sailing; a wet, cold one soon begins to feel the effects not only of prolonged cold but of seasickness too.

• Keep calm at all times. Panic is contagious and frightening to the already nervous child.

• Boost the skipper/owner and show that you have confidence in him and his decisions, thus instilling the same confidence in the children.

• Keep a selection of games, books, puzzles as an emergency stock for really bad days. Bring them out as a surprise when all else seems to have failed.

• Keep a watchful eye open for the first stages of seasickness. Try an anti-sickness tablet, a few drops of lemon juice or glucose, and cut out fatty foods as much as possible.

• It is not good enough just to wear lifejackets; they must be properly secured at all times. Make the habit completely automatic and teach the children the right way to lace or tie them right from the start.

• A knot which is wrongly tied is dangerous afloat. Any knot a child makes, on its lifejacket or securing the dinghy, must be right. Start by teaching two simple knots like the reef and the round turn and two half hitches, and then enlarge upon them.

• Watch for eyestrain in the glare afloat and for sunburn or windburn. Either can make an otherwise enjoyable cruise a misery.

• Show older children what the lifebelt is for. Demonstrate how it should be thrown and explain why. One day they may see someone in trouble and quick action may be needed.

12 CLOTHES FOR SEAGOING

Seagoing clothing is big business and high fashion, and very much a question of personal taste. Most chandlers have a good and varied selection to choose from. Remember that any sailing suit, whether it is one piece or two, must be completely wind and waterproof. The sailing suit is not expected to give warmth; it is for protection only. Warmth comes from the layers worn underneath, and it is the number of layers not the thickness of individual garments which gives warmth – say the experts.

Once again modern synthetic materials have enabled manufacturers to produce hard-weather sailing gear which will stand up to the most rigorous conditions afloat. Make sure that all seams are welded or treated – stitching alone is not waterproof. Wrists and trouser bottoms should have storm cuffs and the front opening, whether fitted with zip, Velcro or buttons, should have a double or storm fastening of some sort. A great deal of time will be spent sitting in water, or at least on wet seats, so the seat bottom should have a reinforced panel and again the seams should be welded. Neck fastening is just as important, and although hoods are not all that comfortable for looking around and feeling the direction of the wind, they are the only real answer to keeping water from getting down the back of the neck in the worst conditions.

One-piece suits, jackets and trousers, smocks and trousers (bib-type and elastic waisted) all have their followers, but personally I think the two-piece suit, so long as the trousers are the non-bib type, is best all round for women. Anyone who has tried to struggle out of a one-piece or bib-type suit in the confines of the tiny heads compartment when the boat is heeling and sailing hard will agree with me.

When buying a sailing suit remember the layers of clothing which will be worn underneath and make sure it is plenty big enough. Just as important, make sure the trousers are long enough and that the jacket comes well down so there is no chance of a gap in the middle. Ideally the trousers will be elasticated at the waist so that they stretch over all the extra layers easily yet still remain snug. The jacket ideally should have a draw cord at the bottom as well as the neck. Good big pockets in the jackets are vital to take all the oddments one collects, so steer clear of sailing outfits without them.

Choose a colour that will show up – light colours stand out at night and yellow, orange and red show up best in the water. Fluorescent strips can be

Typical lightweight waterproofs for the smaller members of the crew. Remember to choose suits big enough to allow for growing and for all the extra layers worn underneath.

bought in various colours and applied to the shoulders, chest, back and arms of oilskins to ensure that they can be spotted in the dark. In any case, make sure it is a colour you feel happy in. A seasick person in green or blue looks ghastly.

Personal buoyancy

There are a wide range of lifejackets, lifevests and buoyancy aids on the market. (Note: see Chapter 11 which explains the basic differences between lifejackets and buoyancy aids.) Some are inflated orally and/or by CO_2 gas, others have built-in safety harnesses. Have a good look at all the various models available at your local chandler and ask for advice for the most suitable for your particular needs.

Some sailing jackets incorporate their own built-in buoyancy in one form or other, some with trapped-in air or foam-filled pockets; others which are fully inflatable. These ease the problem of personal buoyancy to some extent since the jacket with its own built-in buoyancy is in effect two garments in one. Each time the jacket is put on the buoyancy is put on, and there is no problem about deciding when conditions warrant a buoyancy aid. However, in most cases the jackets are swimming aids only. The exception is when the inflatable jacket is worn fully inflated. In this case the buoyancy is there, but the jacket is probably too bulky for active and comfortable wear on a small cruiser. Obviously a compromise has to be reached.

The question of choosing a comfortable garment is just as important for grown-ups as it is for children. An active, busy life on deck and just as active and busy a life in the confined space below make lack of bulk of paramount importance, so a lot of time should be spent in searching for the different types available, trying them on for comfort and then deciding which offer the best protection for the sort of cruising planned, while still considering ease of stowing below.

Perhaps the ideal in small cruisers, whether you venture far offshore or not, is to have a buoyancy aid for each member of the crew (either built into a sailing jacket or as a separate garment) and an approved lifejacket for real emergency. This is the ideal, but if it is not possible then perhaps a lifejacket for non-swimmers and buoyancy aid for swimmers should be the aim.

Safety harnesses

Some sailing suits and jackets are available with built-in safety harnesses or harness fittings, but ideally there should be a safety harness on board for each

Freo suits from Henri-Lloyd for offshore and coastal sailing have triple layered hand taped seams. Among the interesting features are collars with integral throat adjustments, removable soft fabric neck linings, and trousers which are cut away under the arms to give the highest possible fit. Optional extras for the jackets are flotation linings and lifejacket attachment points.

member of the crew. These should be used at the skipper's discretion. All the crew should know where they are stowed and how they work. Non-swimmers should be encouraged to wear them as a matter of course at night or when working on deck in choppy conditions. Everyone on board should also know where the strong points for attaching the lines are to be found and should practise wearing the harness and moving around on deck from one attachment to another in quiet weather in readiness for the real test.

Clothes for warmth

Underneath layers should never be tight – clothes which allow a passage of air around the body give better warmth, and keeping warm afloat is the aim. Coldness brings in its train seasickness, depression and tiredness, and no one suffering in this way can really pull their weight. Clothes for wearing afloat must be chosen wisely; there is a limit to how much you can carry. Special polar undersuits are available but the normal track suit serves equally well and is ideal for lounging below. Warm tights, trousers and long sweaters which come well down over the hips make up the basic below-sailing-wear, and it is a good idea to include a lightweight windproof top for the less arduous days. Warm gloves, socks and a good warm hat – preferably one that can be pulled right down over the ears – and good non-slip deck shoes make up the essentials for keeping warm afloat. The shoes should be a size bigger than normal to take those extra thick socks, and a towelling neck scarf, sun hat and sunglasses to protect against glare should complete the kit.

A complete change of clothing is the ideal as well as various extras for going ashore – but how much depends on the amount of stowage space available. Many crews keep their normal sailing gear handy in canvas holdalls which can be tucked into odd corners, stowing only any special shoregoing gear in lockers and hanging spaces.

13 FIRST AID AND SANITATION
A caution

(Any advice given in the following chapter is at best minimal and superficial, dealing with only a very few of the possible medical emergencies which may confront any of us, anywhere, afloat or ashore. Local St John's Ambulance and Red Cross Societies everywhere offer free training in first aid for the asking.)

Unless the mate knows a limited amount about handling the yacht the skipper is in a very vulnerable position indeed. Just imagine what might happen if he were hit on the head and knocked unconscious – even for a few minutes. It was the thought of this sort of emergency which, more than anything else, prompted me to write this book.

A mate who cruises regularly should be able to cope if left in sole charge. Heave the boat to, keep her quietly jogging along while tending the wounded, keep her on course, free from danger until help is at hand or get safely back to port if necessary. Perhaps run the ship smoothly, under guidance, if the skipper was unlucky enough to break a limb. These are the extreme emergencies, but they could happen and the mate should be aware of them, discuss them and better still work out a plan of action for meeting them, and practise it.

This is looking on the blackest side. More often than not only a first aid kit is needed for minor troubles since the family cruiser is not usually at sea long enough for the more serious ailments to occur.

Lack of space, particularly in the galley, is the cause of many minor accidents below deck, and it is here where a bit of forethought can reduce the risk of mishaps. Most likely are scalds and burns from the stove, and this is why the cook has supreme rights when busy in the galley of a smaller cruiser. Sudden lurches as the ship moves make the likelihood of scalds from hot water, hot dishes and hot fat very real, and it is a good idea to wear waterproof trousers when cooking in a seaway if the weather is very rough. Pans should never be more than half full, and the cook should always check to make sure the stove is free to swing and that the fiddle rails grip the pans securely. Oven gloves are useful too.

After one or two trips afloat and one or two minor accidents we soon learn what can go wrong and what steps can be taken to guard against them. It becomes instinctive to check before opening back hatches and doors in case fingers are trapped, to keep steps and entrances clear and dry so that they do not become skid traps, and second nature to empty hot pans and kettles as soon as they come off the stove and before they can tip and scald the unwary.

Minor accidents, particularly finger-catching ones, are much more likely to happen on deck, but here again familiarity brings confidence. Knowing the correct way to handle ropes, sheets, winches, anchors, engine, warps and lines is the criterion. Handled right, accidents hardly ever occur; handled wrongly the consequences can be very painful indeed.

The sort of ailments likely to be encountered are headaches, stings, sore throats, toothache, septic spots, boils, food poisoning, eye troubles, sunburn, hay fever, constipation, colds, chills, seasickness, splinters, cuts, abrasions, burns, scalds, fainting and so on; an impressive enough list, but they are the sort of troubles dealt with every day ashore and well within the scope of the first aid kit.

The first aid kit

Complete first aid kits are available to buy and many good chandlers stock them – some specifically for boats, in plastic containers and capable of being fitted on the bulkhead. Some also include fire extinguishers – again with special bulkhead mounting which ensures the kit is readily available at all times. There is no point in having the kit tucked away out of sight and difficult to find.

For those who prefer to make up their own boxes the first aid kit might well start with the following, which can be altered and added to as time goes on. This is suggested as the very minimum to cope with the eventualities likely to arise:

Waterproof dressing	Hot water bottle	Sterilized dressings
Insect repellant	Burn dressings	Antidote to bites
Crepe bandage	Oil of cloves	Triangular bandage
Calomine	Cotton wool	Suntan lotion
Sterilized lint	Aspirin	1″ adhesive strip
Seasickness tablets	Finger stall	Laxative
Antiseptic	Indigestion relief	Antiseptic ointment
Eye lotion	Throat/mouth tablets	Eye bath
Scissors	Hayfever antidote	Splinter forceps
Brandy	Safety pins	Chlorodyne
Lip salve	Thermometer	Nail file

Choose a plastic box to keep the first aid equipment in, preferably an airtight one.

Professional attention is needed for more serious accidents like broken bones, dislocations, deep cuts and gashes, serious burns, high temperatures, etc., after the initial first aid treatment.

Here are some suggested cures for troubles likely to arise:

Diarrhoea Half a teaspoon Chlorodyne every six hours until symptoms cease.

Toothache (if due to cavity) Clean out with a toothpick and cotton wool and pack with cotton wool soaked in oil of cloves. Aspirins will help, as will hot and cold face packs if the tooth is infected.

Eyes If a foreign body cannot be removed easily leave it alone. Wash with eye lotion; one part water one part salt water. If the eye is really painful cover it with a pad and rest it.

Food poisoning Dilute as much as possible by swallowing large quantities of water. Induce vomiting by drinking salted water or tickling the back of the throat. Treat for shock and keep warm. Afterwards give a good laxative. No solid food until the patient is better.

Fainting Sit with the head between the knees. Loosen clothing around the neck. Treat for shock, and give hot stimulants.

Shock Lie down, with head low. Wrap warmly and give hot tea/coffee providing there is no head injury or serious bleeding. Never give stimulants if the patient is unconscious, but keep them warm.

Sprains Bathe in cold water for a good half hour. Dry and bind firmly, but not firmly enough to stop circulation. Rest the strained area.

Burns

Minor (i.e., no breaking of skin) Run under cold water to relieve pain. Apply a burn dressing lightly.

More severe burns Treat for shock. Burns which break the skin must be kept moist. Use a burn dressing and bandage lightly. Never prick blisters, and never use oil. Get professional treatment as soon as possible.

Rope burns (caused by ropes running through hands) Extremely painful; treat as heat burns.

Septic spots and boils Apply hot fomentations of boracic lint. Bandage lightly and repeat every three or four hours until there is no discharge. Then apply lint.

Sunburn In normal cases an application of calomine night and morning gives quick relief. Keep covered and away from the sun's rays, and use a protective cream before exposure to the sun again.

Dislocation Dislocations need professional care as soon as possible. As a temporary relief cold may be applied to the joint but do not attempt to re-set. Support the limb in the most comfortable position, bound to the body or in a sling and loosen clothing around the injury.

Fractures

Toes Leave alone.

Fingers Apply a small splint and fix in place with Elastoplast.

Small bones (feet and hands) Immobilize as far as possible with Elastoplast.

Larger bones Immobilize with splints or a sling to prevent pain and shock. Professional attention is needed as soon as possible.

Gippy tummy Keep warm. Dose with Chlorodyne, as directed. Give warm drinks.

Small wounds Small wounds which do not bleed readily should be washed with antiseptic then covered with a sterilized dressing and bound. Keep well clear of salt water, which makes them sore and delays healing.

More serious cuts Cuts which bleed heavily need thorough attention. Venous bleeding, which wells up in a slow continuous dark red stream, can be stopped, whereas arterial bleeding must be stopped by pressure which is applied to the appropriate pressure point before dressing. If this is not sufficient a tourniquet may be needed. Remember that the tourniquet must be loosened every fifteen minutes, even if the bleeding starts again, otherwise more serious damage will result. Professional attention is needed without delay.

Seasickness Seasickness is the most common ailment of all. Luckily for most it is only a temporary malaise. If it persists lie down, rest and keep warm. Take anti-sickness tablets and keep liquid intake to a minimum. Dry biscuits are the safest bet if some sort of food is needed.

The above ailments are mostly obvious even to the layman but other situations, although obviously serious, may be beyond diagnosis by ordinary folk. Above all keep calm and do not panic. If the skipper has been incapacitated make sure that the yacht is safe before dropping everything to attend to him. If there is room heave-to, roll up the jib, free the mainsheet and let the boat drift, or anchor if it is shallow enough.

Do you need a doctor?

Is the casualty conscious, in a state of collapse, bleeding severely, or suffering severe chest pains? In fact, knowing the casualty, have you any suspicions concerning these symptoms?

If unconscious and pinching *both* ear lobes does not get a response check for breathing with your ear to his mouth, look for chest movement. If you cannot detect breathing begin artificial resuscitation immediately.

Severe abdominal pain and a rapid pulse and breathing, clammy skin and sweating suggest internal bleeding and an urgent need for medical help. Similarly severe pain in the centre of the chest and perhaps the neck and left arm *may* indicate a heart attack with similar urgency.

This is a clear case where a distress call on VHF is indicated, not a MAYDAY signature, however, but a PAN PAN MEDICO call. Correctly you would direct your PAN PAN MEDICO call to the nearest Coast radio station, remembering that unlike MAYDAY you would not send the entire message on Channel 16, but would give a working channel such as say 26 or 28 which you propose to use. You would thereafter be put in touch with a doctor who would assess the situation and set in motion such assistance as might be needed. All of which shows yet again how useful it would be for a mate to be able to use the VHF radio with confidence.

If the casualty is unconscious or in a state of collapse while calling for help, he *should not* be left lying on his back, a position which can prove fatal. Instead turn him to lie on his side, one knee slightly raised, one arm extended behind and the other crooked at shoulder level, face on one cheek. This 'coma' position ensures that the casualty can continue to breathe.

Again let me stress that first aid at this level of urgency demands not only written theory but practical training too, however brief.

Hypothermia

Unfortunately a small yacht in the cooler latitudes is an environment particularly at risk, frequently subjecting crews to long periods of cold and dampness. Although most people connect hypothermia with the aftermath of falling overboard, indeed rightly so, the deep chilling of the body can occur without becoming completely soaked. A person can start by loss of body heat through violent seasickness, and in preferring to stay on deck in the fresh air, perhaps inadequately clad, become colder and colder until they suffer from exposure which is the first stage of hypothermia.

Mental and physical lethargy, blurred vision, slurred speech as if drunk and violent fits of shivering are typical. Strangely also there may be sudden fits of energy. The casualty may become grey-faced and cramped.

DO NOT give alcohol, DO NOT try to get the casualty exercising to get warm and DO NOT try rubbing as a means of warming him. Get the sufferer below out of the wind, strip off wet clothing and get him into a sleeping bag with a warm, *not hot*, water bottle or better still with another fit person sharing the sleeping bag. Warm up the boat by putting the stove on if there is one or by starting the engine with the engine box open. The aim is to make the most of the casualty's own body heat plus warming from the outside. A large plastic bag pulled on over the sleeping bag will help with the former and keeping the head lower than the feet also helps.

No chapter on first aid and safety would be complete without some mention of artificial resuscitation. Anyone who goes to sea or, in fact, any visitor to the seashore, might be called upon to offer assistance of this sort at some time, and it is wise to have some idea of what to do if an emergency should arise.

The expired air method (mouth to mouth or nose) is considered the most effective since it can be carried out by one person and produces better ventilation to the lungs than the manual methods. This is vitally important because lack of oxygen in the blood supply to the brain causes irreparable damage to the nerve cells in a matter of minutes. This is why resuscitation, whichever method is used, must be given as quickly as possible.

NOTE: Present day fear of AIDS raises problems with any form of mouth-to-mouth resuscitation. Special lip guards are available to overcome this.

The following tips are extracted from the Royal Life Saving Society's booklet *Artificial Respiration*. The Society stresses that although its inclusion might save lives, this description is *not* a substitute for proper instruction.

How to carry out expired air resuscitation:

1) Lay the patient on his back and, if on a slope, have the stomach slightly lower than the chest.

2) Make a brief inspection of the mouth and throat to ensure that they are clear of obvious obstruction.

3) Give the patient's head the maximum backwards tilt so that the chin is prominent, the mouth closed and the neck stretched to give clear airway.

4) Open your mouth wide, make an airtight seal over the nose of the patient and blow. The operator's cheek or the hand supporting the chin can be used to seal the patient's lips.

5) *Or*, if the nose is blocked, open the patient's mouth using the hand supporting the chin, open your mouth wide and make an airtight seal over his mouth and blow. This may also be used as an alternative to the mouth-to-nose technique even when the nose is not blocked, in which case the nostrils must be sealed with the operator's cheek or by moving the hand holding the top of the patient's head so that the fingers can be used to pinch the nostrils. The wrist must be kept low on the patient's forehead to ensure that the full tilt of the head is maintained. If the patient's mouth cannot be opened, blow through his parted lips as the air passing between his teeth may be sufficient to inflate his lungs.

6) After exhaling, turn your head to watch for chest movement whilst inhaling deeply in readiness to blow again.

7) If the chest does not rise, check that the patient's mouth and throat are free of obstruction and the head is tilted backwards as far as possible. Blow again.

8) If air enters the patient's stomach through blowing too hard, press the stomach gently, with the head of the patient turned to one side.

9) Commence resuscitation with six quick inflations of the patient's chest to give a rapid build-up of oxygen in the patient's blood and then slow down to twelve to fifteen respirations per minute or blow again each time the patient's chest has deflated.

   With small children and babies, inflation at the rate of twenty a minute is achieved by a series of puffs, each one ceasing as the chest starts to rise. *Under no circumstances blow violently into a baby's lungs.*

10) Whilst preparing to commence resuscitation breathe deeply with the mouth open to build up the oxygen content.

Sanitation afloat

Ventilation of the cabin cannot be too highly stressed. People live, eat, sleep, wash and use the toilet in a very confined space, so cleanliness and good ventilation are essential. Ideally there should be a ventilator over the toilet and one over the galley as well.

Salt water is an excellent disinfectant and luckily there's no shortage of it, so make certain the toilet is really well flushed out after use. The discharge pump to the toilet is very delicate; do not mince words – make sure everybody on board knows just how delicate it is and spell out all the items which will block it. Better still produce a list of do's and don'ts for the toilet and stick it up in the compartment where it is in clear view. Even matches, hair grips, tooth paste tops, etc., can block it, and since the toilet compartment is usually used for washing too it is very easy for something to slip into the pan. If anything does get into the pan, enlist the skipper's help immediately – in no circumstances try to pump it through.

Being so delicate the marine WC cannot take sanitary towels, disposable nappies, cotton wool etc. This must be a hard and fast rule. Care can guarantee a trouble-free life; carelessness can cause unlimited trouble and discomfort for all. Use the special toilet cleaners supplied for marine use and always pump some into the pipes when leaving the yacht for some time to ensure the pipes stay fresh.

GLOSSARY OF NAUTICAL TERMS USED

Abaft: behind.

Aboard: on board or in a vessel.

About: go on the opposite tack.

Aground: when the keel sits on the bottom.

Aloft: up the mast or in the rigging.

Amidships: in the centre of the vessel, from bow to stern or across.

Anchor (arm): one half of the curved part of a fisherman anchor.

Anchor (cable): a rope, chain or combination of both joining yacht to anchor.

Anchor (chocks): special fittings on deck to which the anchor is secured when not in use.

Anchor (fluke): part of the anchor which digs into the ground.

Anchor (kedge): smaller supplementary anchor.

Anchor (scope): the length of cable used.

Anchor (weighing): the act of raising the anchor.

Anchor (windlass): a geared winch for hauling in an anchor cable.

Apparent wind: the wind as experienced by a moving object as opposed to a stationary one.

Backing (sails): hauling the clew of the sail to windward, which helps to turn the bow quickly.

Backstay: wire/rope leading aft from the mast to stop it bending forward.

Battens: stiffeners fitted in a sail to stop the leech flapping.

Beam: maximum breadth of vessel.

Bearing away: putting the helm to windward to turn the vessel away from the wind.

Bearings (by eye): direction of an object from where the observer is standing.

Bearings (compass): direction according to the compass card.

Bearings (transit): marks in line.

Beating: to tack, to sail a zigzag course upwind with the wind first on one bow then the other.

Bending on (sails): to fit sails to the mast and spars ready for hoisting.

Berth: a mooring place in a dock or marina.

Bilge: space in a vessel beneath the sole (the floor).

Boathook: a staff with hook at one end for picking up moorings or floating objects.

Boom: horizontal spar for extending the foot, or bottom, of a sail.

Bow: front of a vessel.

Broadside on: sideways on.

Bulkhead: upright partition dividing the hull into several compartments.

Bunks: sleeping berths.

Bunks (leeboards, also lee cloths, lee canvas): a removable board or taut canvas screen to prevent a sleeper falling out of a bunk.

Boarding ladder: portable steps of wood, metal or rope with wooden steps hung down the side of the yacht.

Bow fender: a 'Y' shaped pad to protect the bows from abrasion by anchor or mooring chain.

Buoy: floating marker for moorings, underwater obstructions and channels.

Buoyancy aid: as distinct from lifejacket which always supports head and face above water, an aid usually in waistcoat form which provides body support while swimming.

Burgee: triangular flag flown at the masthead showing the club to which the owner belongs.

Cable: anchor chain or rope.

Capsize: overturn, upset.

Chart (datum): theoretical level from which the height and depth are measured. Roughly the lowest level to which an ordinary tide is likely to fall.

Chart (scale): the proportion of actual distance represented on the chart.

Claw ring: a device involving rollers to which the mainsheet of a roller boom is attached.

Cleat: wood or metal fitting to which rope may be secured without tying – usually by figure-of-eight turns.

Clew (of sail): lower after corner.

Close-hauled: sailing as close to the wind as possible.

Close reach: point of sailing midway between reaching and close-hauled.

Coachroof: part of the deck raised to give extra headroom.

Cockpit: well near the stern in which the helmsman sits.

Companionway: entry from the deck or cockpit to the accommodation.

Compass (bearing): direction according to the compass card.

Compass (course): directional heading taken from a bearing by magnetic compass.

Compasses: instruments for maintaining direction or taking bearings. All have a card with a magnetic north-seeking pole which is free to revolve in fluid.

Crane lines: short tie-backs used to stop rigging tapping against the mast.

Crosstrees (or spreaders): struts projecting laterally from a mast to spread apart the upper or 'cap' shrouds.

Dan-buoy: buoy used as a marker having an upright flag pole and counterweight.

Decca: electronic navigation system based on a network of automatic radio beacons.

Deck head: underside of deck.

Deviation: compass error caused by nearby iron, etc., deflecting the north-seeking magnet from its alignment.

Dinghy: ship's tender, small open boat used for ferrying between vessel and shore.

Distress flares: pyrotechnic signals for summoning help in trouble.

Downhaul: ropes for pulling down sails or boom.

Down tide: at a point from the observer in the direction to which the tide is running.

Drifting: moving with the tide or wind only.

Ebb tide: the dropping or receding tide.

Echo sounder: electronic device for showing the depth of water under a vessel.

Fairlead: bullseye or fitting through which a rope is passed to alter the direction of lead or keep it clear of fittings, etc.

Fathom: nautical measure of 6 feet.

Fenders (fendoffs): pads of rubber, rope or cork for protecting the vessel when going alongside quays or other vessels.

Fend off: push off any obstruction which is liable to cause damage.

Fiddles: strips, usually wood, fitted to tables, ledges etc., to stop things sliding off. Also metal or wood bars fitted to fixed stoves to keep pans secure.

Fin keel: a ballasted keel in the form of a deep blade or fin.

Finger pier: narrow walkway projecting from a marina pontoon.

Fitting out: the yearly overhaul and spring clean of a vessel.

Flood tide: rising tide.

Following sea: waves travelling in the same direction as the vessel.

Foot (of sail): lower edge.

Foredeck: front part of the deck over the fo'c'sle.

Forehatch: deck access to the fo'c'sle.

Foresail: headsail, hanked or rolled round the forestay.

Forestay: wire/rope leading from the bow to the masthead.

Fo'c'sle (forecastle): part of the accommodation beneath the foredeck.

Foul tide: unfavourable tide, going in the opposite direction to the vessel.

Galley: the ship's kitchen.

Gel coat: a glassfibre hull consists of multiple layers of glass matting or chips impregnated with resin and protected by a hard, glossy colour coat or gel.

Genoa: large triangular headsail for use in lighter airs.

Gimbals: system of keeping stove, lamps, compass, etc. swinging as the boat moves so that the item is always level.

Going about: altering course into the wind from one tack to the other.

Grab rails: handholds on the coachroof and elsewhere.

Grid compass: magnetic steering compass fitted with movable ring which has parallel lines on it. The compass card has a corresponding line which must be kept in alignment.

Guardrails: form of safety fence around the deck.

Gybe: transfer the mainsail from one side of the vessel to the other when running.

Halliards: ropes with which sails are hoisted.

Hand-bearing compass: portable compass fitted with a prism through which bearings of objects may be read by sight.

Hanks (or hanked): metal or plastic fittings by which sails are attached to masts or booms or hoisted up stays.

Harden in (sails): haul in sheets to flatten sails.

Head (of sail): top corner of a sail which is hoisted up a mast or stay.

Heading up: turning the bow of the vessel nearer to the wind.

Headroom: distance in a vessel between floor and deckhead.

Heads: the marine toilet, so called because it is usually right up in the bow (or head) of the vessel.

Headsails: triangular sails set forward of the mast.

Head sea: waves, breakers, coming from the direction in which it is desired to sail.

Head to wind: vessel facing directly into the wind.

Headway: progress of a vessel through the water.

Head wind: wind blowing in the direction in which it is desired to sail.

Heave-to: trim helm and sails so that the vessel remains almost stationary.

Heaving line: light line, usually with a knob on the end, thrown to make contact between the vessel and the shore when going alongside, etc.

Heel: lean over.

Helm: tiller or wheel used for steering. The tiller is usually a metal or wooden bar fitted to the rudder head.

High water: the time at which a flood tide reaches its highest point.

Hoisting: raising, lifting sails, anchor, etc.

Hull: body of the vessel, excluding mast and gear.

IALA: International Association of Lighthouse Authorities. IALA system 'A' combines two systems of buoyage based upon the principle of 'red to port' and covers most of the world except North, South and Central America, Japan, South Korea and the Philippines. System 'B', 'red to starboard' covers the remainder.

Inflatable (dinghy): an air-inflated dinghy.

Jib: foremost headsail.

Kicking strop: a short but powerful tackle or hydraulic strut which holds down the boom.

Knot: measure of speed. One knot = one nautical mile = 6080 feet per hour.

Lashed down: tied down securely.

Latitude: distance north or south of the equator, expressed in degrees.

Lead line: weight on a marked line used to find depth of water.

Leech (of sail): aftermost edge of a sail.

Lee side: side opposite to that on which the wind is blowing.

Leeward: any point downwind of the observer.

Lifebuoy: circular or horseshoe shaped float – usually big enough to encircle a man's chest.

Lifejacket: designed to support the wearer on his back, face above water.

Lifelines: rope or wire passed through uprights along the line of the deck to protect crew from falling overboard.

Liferaft: an automatically inflating, usually circular, raft with a protective canopy for emergency use.

Longitude: distance in degrees east or west of the meridian of Greenwich.

Long keel: usually found on traditional designs of boat. It may extend three-quarters of the length of the hull.

Loran (Long Range Aid to Navigation): an American position-finding system.

Low water: lowest point of the tide.

Lubber line: mark on the compass bowl which corresponds with the ship's head.

Luff (of sail): forward edge of a sail.

Luffing: bringing the vessel so close to the wind that the sail starts to flutter.

Magnetic north: direction in which magnetic North Pole at present lies.

Mainsail: the principal sail.

Mainsheet: a powerful tackle or system of blocks and ropes controlling the lateral movement of the mainsail.

Make fast: to secure a rope.

Marina: yacht harbour. Boats usually lie alongside pontoons or each other, and toilets, water etc., are provided.

Mast: a spar set upright on a deck to support rigging and sails.

Mayday: international distress call. Only used when a vessel is in grave and *imminent* danger requiring *immediate* assistance.

Mooring: permanent anchoring equipment laid on the seabed to keep a vessel floating in one position.

Mooring (buoy): buoy supporting a mooring chain with a ring above and below to which a vessel is moored.

Mooring up: the act of securing a vessel to a mooring, or by means of various lines to a quay, pier, jetty or another vessel.

Neap tides: tides which rise and fall least. Opposite to spring tides.

Painter: rope attached to the bow of a dinghy by which it is towed along or secured to a vessel, quay etc.

Pan pan: urgent call. Danger not imminent. Assistance not immediately required.

Pan pan medico: urgent radio call for medical assistance.

Parallel rules: rules used in navigation, designed so that they can be moved around on the chart with the edges always parallel.

Port tack: sailing close-hauled with wind striking the sails on the port (or left) side.

Port: left side of the ship looking forward. Signified by red light. Opposite to starboard.

Pram hood: a hinged awning above the companionway acting as a windbreak and shelter.

Pulpit: tubular stainless steel rail at the bow and stern.

Quarter: part of the vessel from midway to the stern. Thus either port or starboard quarter.

Quarter berth: bunk running under the side of the cockpit.

Rafting up: a practice whereby a number of yachts lie alongside each other next to a jetty, or swinging on a mooring or posts.

Reaching: sailing at right angles to the wind.

Reefing: reducing the size of the sail, usually by rolling it round the boom, mast or stay.

Reefing (pennants): short ropes for pulling the sail down to the boom when reefing a mainsail.

Reefing (slab): a system of reducing the size of the mainsail by taking a large tuck in the bottom.

Riding light: all-round white light shown when at anchor.

Rigging: (running): halliards for hoisting sails, sheets for trimming sails etc.

Rigging (standing): wire and/or rope used to support the mast and spars.

Roller jib: a sail stowing system similar in principle to a roller blind.

Roller reefing: a rotating boom which reduces the mainsail by rolling it up.

Rudder: a blade fitted to the stern by which a vessel is steered.

Running: sailing downwind.

Safety harness: webbing harness with line and snap-hook attached to minimize the risk of falling overboard.

Sail area: total measurement of normal sails.

Saloon: main living space in a vessel.

Sat nav: Automated position finding electronics based on the regular passage of satellites.

Scope: length of cable by which a vessel is anchored.

Seacock: taps shutting off pipes which pass through the hull.

Sea miles: one nautical mile = approx 1.15 land miles.

Seaway: exposed and broken water.

Seizing end: to secure or to bind ends of ropes or two parts of the same rope together.

Separation zones: designated sea areas dividing shipping lanes.

Setting (sails): hoisting sails ready for sailing.

Sheets: rope attached to the clew of a sail by which it is controlled.

Sheet winches revolving drums giving added power for hauling in jib sheets.

Shipping lanes: a means of separating shipping into one-way tracks, similar to a motorway.

Slack tide: short period at the turn of the tide when there is no tidal stream.

Snubbing (anchor): stopping the chain running suddenly so that it jerks.

Sounding: measuring the depth of water under the vessel.

Spill wind: to turn closer to the wind so that the wind is shaken out of the sails.

Spinnaker: large parachute-like triangular sail of light fabric used for running.

Spray dodgers: fabric screens flanking the cockpit, usually carrying the yacht's name.

Spray hood: (see pram hood).

Spring tides: those which rise and fall most. Opposite to neap tides.

Springs: mooring lines which prevent pivoting movement.

Stanchions: posts fitted round the deck to hold lifelines.

Starboard: right hand side of a vessel when looking forward. Signified by green light. Opposite to port.

Starboard tack: sailing close-hauled with wind blowing over the starboard side.

Staysail: the inner headsail of a two headsail rig.

Steering by compass: maintaining a course by keeping the compass card on a selected heading.

Steerage way: having sufficient forward movement for the rudder to work.

Stern: back of a vessel.

Stern ladder: a permanent folding ladder fixed to the stern.

Stowage (sails): taking sails down, either right off the spars or securing them to the boom. Rolling them round a boom, or stay.

Surging: relieving tension on a rope by allowing it to slip, under control.

Swifter line: a means of preventing halliards from flapping against the mast by tying them to forward shrouds.

Tacks, tacking: beating to windward in a zigzag manner with the wind first on one bow then the other.

Tack tackle: pulley attached to the luff of a sail which allows it to be pulled taut.

Tackle: an arrangement of pulley blocks and rope which provides extra power.

Take a turn: passing a rope round a cleat, bollard or winch when it is about to come under strain.

Tender: a yacht's dinghy.

Three point bearing: the intersection of three bearings (usually by compass) giving a positive position when plotted on chart.

Tidal range: the distance which the level of the water travels between low water and the succeeding high water.

Tides: rise and fall of the sea under the influence of the moon and sun.

Tide tables: tables showing tidal predictions for the year. These include times of high water and heights of tides.

Tideway: the actual stream of the tide.

Tiller: wood or metal bar secured to the rudder head by means of which a vessel is steered.

Tiller (lashing): a means of preventing movement or fixing a tiller in a chosen position.

Topping lift: wire or rope supporting the outer end of a boom.

Topsides: the area of hull between waterline and deck.

Trimming sails: pulling sails in or letting them out so that they draw to the best advantage.

True north: direction in which geographical north lies.

True wind: the wind as it is felt by a stationary observer at sea level.

Twin keels: a boat having two ballast keels side by side instead of one central keel.

Under way: a vessel is under way when she moves over the ground or through the water.

Up tide: at a point from the observer in the direction from which the tidal stream is running.

VHF radio: Very High Frequency two-way radio of limited range.

Warps: strong rope used for securing alongside, mooring or towing.

Watches: a regular roster of on-duty periods shared by the crew.

Weather side: side of vessel on which wind is blowing. Opposite to lee side.

Whipping: binding the end of a rope to stop it coming unravelled.

Winch: a revolving drum which gives extra power for handling ropes.

Weathercocking: the natural behaviour of a drifting boat, turning her stern into the wind.

Windage: the above-water hull and superstructure which offers resistance to the wind.

Windward: direction from which the wind is blowing.

INDEX